Rese

Biological Clock

- FEEL YOUNGER
- LOOK YOUNGER
- BUILD A YOUNGER BODY

Al Sears M.D.
Medical Direc

Al Sears, MD

Published by:
AhHa Press, Inc.
11903 Southern Blvd., Suite 208
Royal Palm Beach, FL 33411
Phone: 888-795-4005 Fax: 561-784-7851
Website: www.alsearsmd.com and www.mypureradiance.com

Meet Dr. Al Sears

A physician, author, physical trainer and researcher, Al Sears, M.D., is one of today's leading voices in anti-aging medicine and natural health. Dr. Sears has seen over 20,000 patients at his thriving private practice, located in Royal Palm Beach, Florida.

Dr. Sears has written six books and over 500 articles on supplements, alternative medicine, anti-aging and skin. He also publishes the newsletters *Health Confidential, Doctor's House Call* and *Ageless Beauty*. With the publication of *The Doctor's Heart Cure*, Dr. Sears established himself as a leading authority on alternative and natural medicine.

He has since published *High Speed Fat Loss in 7 Easy Steps*, and a revolutionary theory of exercise, *PACE: The 12-Minute Fitness Revolution*. Thousands of readers credit Dr. Sears' PACE program for their return to health and fitness.

Dr. Sears is a member of the American Academy of Anti-Aging Medicine and is Board Certified in Anti-Aging Medicine. He is also the founder and director of The Wellness Research Foundation, a non-profit organization involved in ongoing original research to evaluate natural alternatives to pharmaceutical therapies.

Table of Contents

Part 3: Build a Younger Body

Part 4: Live Younger Longer – Recreate the Body of Your Youth

Introduction

This had such an impact on me, I still remember it: I was sitting at my desk almost 20 years ago. I like to stay abreast of non-medical scientific literature. So I picked up my issue of *Scientific American* and something jumped off the page at me.

Elizabeth Blackburn had made a truly revolutionary discovery. I'll never forget it.

When I read that she'd found a solution to aging *already in our genes*, I took out a piece of paper and wrote down something that I still have today. It says, "This will change the world as we know it."

Now, finally, it seems other people think so, too. This breakthrough won the 2009 Nobel Prize in Physiology or Medicine.

With all the anti-aging "solutions" on the market today, it's hard to know what works and what doesn't. As an anti-aging doctor, I've made it my life's work to sift through the fads, diets, lotions, and other "fixes" to find things that truly work and share them with you.

This discovery is so revolutionary that it changed the way scientists and doctors viewed the aging process. It involves the discovery of telomerase, the key to anti-aging. Telomerase is an enzyme that's found in all of your cells that controls how old your cells act. Once activated, telomerase can actually make your cells – and therefore your body – younger.

With this ongoing research on aging, we have opened new doors to how we can control the aging process. I held a conference that brought together the best minds studying anti-aging and telomerase to show others exactly how this process works and ways it can be triggered into action.

When your cells age, your body becomes weaker. Your joints ache, your mind gets cloudy, and you become more susceptible to things like infection, disease, and other ailments. And old cells make everyday activities harder for your body to handle.

But you've taken the first step to fighting back by reading this book.

Reset Your Biological Clock brings you these scientific breakthroughs and shows you how to apply them to your daily life. I've created this complete, comprehensive guide to help stop – even reverse – the aging process from the inside out so you can feel and look younger, stronger, and more energetic… just like you did when you were in your 20s.

In this book, I'm going to tell you exactly how you can stop old age before it stops you. You can flip the anti-aging switch in your cells using native eating habits, nutrients, natural supplements, and exercise. And by making these few simple changes, you'll feel revitalized, sleep better than ever, have a more robust sex life, and counteract stress and be relaxed and happy.

Conventional medicine has told you how to live a "healthy lifestyle." But if you're following this advice, you're actually taking years off your life.

In this book, you'll be introduced to powerful foods, supplements and the right combination of specific nutrients and antioxidants to re-energize and rejuvenate your body, your skin, and your mind from the inside out. You'll be stronger, more focused, and more able to fight off sickness… even your eyesight can improve. You'll add years to your life.

I've also dedicated a section to skin care. Many of the cosmetics available on the market today contain damaging chemicals that cause your skin to age. I show you natural solutions to counteract the damage, and reduce the signs of aging dramatically.

And I've included a chapter on exercise that can turn back the hands of time – and turn your body into a fat-burning furnace. I show you how standard exercise (like jogging, running, and cardio) can actually make you weaker and age more quickly. With my program, called PACE, you won't have to spend hours at the gym or do endless cardio workouts ever again. Instead of damaging your body, you'll be training it to burn fat, increase your lungpower and build a bigger, stronger heart.

From body- and skin-nourishing nutrition to anti-aging exercises and new, noninvasive technology, this book gives you strategies to help you identify the optimal lifestyle to look and feel great while increasing your longevity.

I hope you'll use this book as a reference for proven ways to help you look and feel younger.

I've divided the book into four parts: (1) Grow Younger; (2) Feel Younger; (3) Look Younger; and (4) Live Younger. This is to make it easier for you to find the specific information you need in any given moment.

Although each part contains strategies for slowing or reversing the aging process, you don't have to apply all the tips and secrets to look and feel younger for years to come. Just read through the book and pick the strategies and tips from each section that feel right for you. That way you'll create your own formula for longevity and a timeless, ageless look.

PART 1
Grow Younger
Reset Your Biological Clock

A Stunning Discovery That Allows You to Reverse Aging

I know the whole concept of being able to grow younger goes against everything you've ever heard before.

But, if you're willing to open your mind and suspend your skepticism for a few moments, you'll learn about a remarkable discovery that can change everything you think you know about aging.

What is this discovery?

It's a hidden switch that's in every cell of your body. This switch controls how long you live... and when you die. It even has the power to extend your life – maybe indefinitely.

Most doctors have never heard of it.

A group of scientists stumbled upon it just 10 years ago. They watched in awe as generation after generation of cells multiplied... *without aging.*

As one top researcher put it in a Harvard report, "with this switch turned on, these cells become 'immortalized.'"

Until very recently, we didn't know how to activate it. Today we do.

We've uncovered the natural mechanism in your body that sets aging in motion. And we've found ways to flip the switch, bringing it to a halt.

For the first time ever, you can slow down and even reverse aging.

Imagine...

- Hitting the "century mark"... with energy to burn

- Watching your great-great-grandchildren grow up... and having the strength and vigor to keep up with them, every step of the way

- Leading a rich, active life well into your "twilight years"... out on the golf course, working in the garden, visiting with family and friends

It's not just fantasy. Today, new research made it a reality.

Before I can explain how to flip the switch, there's something you need to understand ...

How to Tinker With the Aging Process

Not long ago, I held my first conference on something called "telomere biology." People from all over the country attended the event, and they all walked away with the ability to control their aging clock and add years of abundant health to their lives.

I've got to get a little technical here, but bear with me for a minute. Understanding how telomeres work will help you understand how to activate your hidden anti-aging switch.

Telomeres are "caps" at the ends of every cell's DNA. They act like the plastic fittings on the ends of your shoelaces, and keep your DNA strands from fraying.

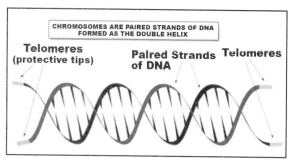

Telomeres are a measure of your body's true biological age. When your telomeres get shorter and shorter over time, they're no longer able to protect your DNA.

This robs you of your vitality and leaves you vulnerable to those dreaded signs of aging.

Shortened telomeres dramatically boost your risk of serious diseases. One study of 60- to 75-year-olds showed those with short telomeres had a 300% higher death rate from heart disease. They also had an 800% higher death rate from infectious diseases.

Worse, when your telomeres completely run down, cell division stops. And that's even more disastrous. Because when new cells no longer replace damaged ones, you die.

But now we know how you can tinker with this process ... and live to be over 100 years old while keeping all the strength, vitality, and youth you had when you were in your 20s.

The Greatest Breakthrough in Anti-Aging Medicine

It involves the enzyme telomerase. And it just happens to be the most exciting advancement in anti-aging medicine ever. In fact, the scientists who uncovered it were recently awarded the 2009 Nobel Prize in Physiology or Medicine.

Here's what they discovered:

There's a gene in your body that activates your telomerase enzyme.

It acts like a genetic switch. It can stop the shortening of telomeres and even re-grow them. But this genetic switch turns off when you're born.

Can you guess what this genetic switch is?

That's right; it's the hidden switch I told you about a minute ago.

Now for the first time, the emerging science of telomere biology has found a way to turn this genetic switch back *on*.

It's a breakthrough supplement – a natural extract that comes from the Astragalus plant, and it activates your telomerase gene.

That means you can actually stop, and even reverse your body's aging process!

I'm very excited about this telomerase activator and have been spreading the word as much as possible. The implications are enormous, because ...

Now You Don't Have to Grow Old If You Don't Want to

Most people think of genes only as components that determine basic body features like hair, skin, and eye color. But they do much more than that. Your genes also play a role in your health and chronic disease.

How your genes express themselves has a profound effect on your future. If you control how your genes express themselves, then, in theory, you can turn on genes that lengthen your life and turn off genes that lead to chronic diseases.

This ground-breaking supplement affects genes related to aging and cell division, keeping your telomeres from shortening, so you can live a longer and healthier life.

If you have the time and the resources, this breakthrough therapy is a great way to go. But there are also many other all-natural ways to help prevent your telomeres from shortening.

How to Get Your Body to Work Like a Well-Oiled Machine Again

Most everyone I know gets a big thrill when somebody pegs their age as much younger than it truly is. Someone thinking they're just five years younger can put a smile on their face for days.

But did you know that people who *look* younger than their age also live a longer and healthier life than those who look older than their years?

It's true!

Researchers have discovered the younger your perceived age is, the more likely it is that you'll have an extended lifespan.

In a long-term study involving 913 pairs of twins, Danish researchers discovered that the twins who looked younger than their true age had better health and longer survival rates than their older-looking siblings. And the larger the difference in perceived age, the more likely it was that the older-looking twin died first.

What's the secret?

The people who looked younger had longer telomeres.

Remember, the shorter your telomeres, the faster you age. Cells with shorter telomeres begin to slow down and act old.

Eventually, the damage makes you age more quickly. So you look older, feel older, and are more vulnerable to age-related diseases and death.

Research shows that people who live to a very old age have inherited genes that allow them to maintain telomere length more effectively.

At the same time, they experience fewer age-related diseases, like cardiovascular problems and diabetes. These are two of the leading causes of death among older individuals.

But don't worry if you don't have the right genes. A new study published in the *American Journal of Clinical Nutrition* shows that you can take a significant step toward maintaining and extending the length of your telomeres with specific vitamin supplements.

The study showed that people who take a daily multivitamin had younger DNA and had 5.1 percent longer telomeres than non-users. In other words, taking certain vitamins can keep you younger longer.

These All-Stars Help You Reverse Your Genetic Clock

The study was full of good news. It turns out that vitamin B12 supplements increase telomere length. And vitamins C and E increase the lifespan of cells by preventing telomere shortening.

Why are vitamins B12, C, and E so effective at maintaining telomere length?

It's their powerful antioxidant activity. Your telomeres are extremely vulnerable to oxidative stress.

It's always a good idea to start with a diet full of foods that give you as many of the vitamins and minerals that keep you healthy. Here's a list of good food sources of the telomere-supporting vitamins:

Foods Sources of Vitamins B12, C, and E

Vitamin B12	Vitamin C	Vitamin E
Beef (Grass-Fed)	Kiwi	Turnip Greens
Beef Liver	Strawberry	Spinach
Salmon	Orange	Broccoli
Haddock	Grapefruit	Almonds
Tuna	Mango	Peanuts
Trout	Red & Green Bell Peppers	Olive Oil
Milk	Raspberries	Papaya

Of course, these vitamins do a lot more for you than keeping you younger longer. Here are some of their other benefits:

Nutrient	Benefits	Recommendations
Vitamin B12	Slows and reverses aging Builds a healthy heart Fights chronic fatigue Improves neurological function	I recommend taking at least 100 mcg per day. Although, I have advised my patients to take as much as 500 mcg per day or more for improving things like brain function and energy levels.

Nutrient	Benefits	Recommendations
Vitamin C	Helps your cells live longer Fights free radicals before they can do damage Maintains body structure Helps the immune system Aids the nervous system Fights inflammation	Take up to 3,000 mg per day if you're currently in good health. I always recommend pregnant women get at least 6,000 mg per day. Take it with food to avoid an upset stomach. You also want to make sure you get the natural form of vitamin C and not the synthetic form. In one particular study, natural vitamin C was 148% more effective than the synthetic form. And it stayed in the test participants' systems longer.
Vitamin E	Slows the aging process Fights free radicals Lowers risk of heart disease Lowers risk of cancer	Take vitamin E as "mixed tocopherols." Your body is better able to absorb them in their natural, organic "d" form. But many vitamin manufacturers use the inferior synthetic "dl" form. I recommend 400 IU of vitamin E a day.

Your ancestors had no problem getting enough of these nutrients from their foods. Back then, grass-fed cattle were abundant, and it was a great source of B12. And fruits and vegetables were grown in mineral-rich soil, without being poisoned with dangerous fertilizers and pesticides.

But these days, diet alone won't give you the level of vitamins you need to prevent your telomeres from shortening and to maintain your health and longevity. That's why you need to supplement your diet.

Here Are the Doses You Need...

It is possible to get some of these vitamins from your food. But in order to get the anti-oxidant levels, supplements are necessary. For example, antioxidant doses of vitamin E are virtually impossible to get in the diet. You would have to eat 2 pounds of sunflower seeds every day!

Oil-soluble vitamins like vitamin E should be taken in gelcap form. Try to find as many of them as you can together in a single supplement. Take them with a teaspoon of flaxseed oil or peanut butter for best absorption. Or taking them during a meal with fat or oil in it will do the trick.

Taking these antioxidants will help quench oxidative damage and help keep your telomeres from shortening.

Remember: Antioxidants slow age-associated changes to your cells. They will help you look and feel younger, as well.

You can take each of your supplements separately. Or you can take a multivitamin that combines all of these vitamins at these levels.

But if you want to use a multivitamin, shop with caution.

The study I mentioned earlier revealed that iron supplements have a negative effect on telomeres. It causes them to shorten. So you'll want to stay away from any multivitamin that contains iron.

While you're shopping, keep in mind that most brands usually don't contain more than 100% of the U.S. RDA for most nutrients. The RDA is the amount the government recommends you take, but it's not usually enough to lower your risk of serious disease or to have a positive impact on your telomeres.

For example, the RDA for vitamins B12, C, and E for adult males is 2.4 mcg, 90 mg, and 22.5 IU, respectively. These numbers are well below the levels that were found to be beneficial in the study. So you'll need to be a smart shopper when it comes to selecting the right multivitamin.

When looking for a superior multivitamin, you want it to have at least 500 mg of vitamin C. It should also contain 200 IU of vitamin E and 100 mcg of B12. This will give

Keep This in Check for a Healthier Life

Homocysteine is an amino acid that accumulates in your tissues. It's a natural byproduct of cell metabolism – think of it as a "waste product." If your homocysteine levels are high, you're at greater risk for Alzheimer's, Parkinson's, heart disease, and impotence.

There's a reason why: **Researchers have found that people with high homocysteine levels** *tripled the amount of telomere length that was lost during cell division.*[i] No wonder it's linked to so many age-related diseases!

You can measure your homocysteine levels with a simple blood test. And you can lower homocysteine naturally, without drugs. Here's what you should take to keep it in check ... you can find these nutrients at most health-food stores.

(Amounts are daily)
Vitamin B12 – 500 mcg
Folic Acid – 800 mcg
Vitamin B6 – 25 mg
Riboflavin (B2) – 25 mg
TMG (trimethylglycine) – 500 mg

[i] Xu et al. "Homocysteine accelerates endothelial cell senescence." FEBS Letters. 2000. 470:20-24.

you much more than the RDA amounts.

The multivitamins on drugstore and supermarket shelves may not be the best choice for you. They often fall short of the vitamins and minerals you need most. They can also fall short in terms of quality, since many of them are synthetic instead of natural.

Taking a quality multivitamin is an important step to better health for everybody. It's inexpensive and easy to add to your daily routine.

And now, we have proof that taking one can actually help you change your genetic age.

PART 2
Feel Younger
Regain Maximum Vitality by Working From the Inside Out

A Spark Plug for Your Cells ...

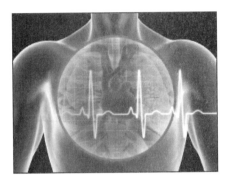

When I was in medical school, a small group of researchers were investigating the anti-aging properties of a newly discovered super-nutrient found in every cell of the human body.

The research was electrifying. It found that Coenzyme Q10 (CoQ10) could be a virtual "fountain of youth" that could ward off chronic health problems while maintaining youthful vigor well into your 60s, 70s, and 80s.

At the time, it sounded like science fiction. But it turned out to be one of the biggest breakthroughs in anti-aging.

You see, CoQ10 gives your cells a constant source of new energy – keeping them working and acting young.

That's crucial to the aging process, because when your cells are starved of energy, they age faster. But keep those cells brimming with fresh fuel, and you can keep the strength, stamina, and endurance of your youth.

CoQ10 has also been shown to ...

- Fire up your aging brain.
- Reinvigorate your heart.
- Sharpen your vision.
- Turbo-charge your immune defenses.

While that's great news, it gets even better.

Ubiquinol Dramatically Slows Aging in Laboratory Tests

Ubiquinol may quickly become one of the preferred treatments in the evolving specialty of anti-aging medicine. That's because preliminary studies suggest that ubiquinol dramatically slows down the aging process.

Japanese researchers gave mice ubiquinol, conventional CoQ10, or a placebo. The mice fed a placebo aged normally. The mice given CoQ10 aged but were slightly more healthy.

But the mice that were given ubiquinol looked and acted like young, healthy mice – despite being the equivalent of 80 years old in human terms. The aging process actually decreased by 51%.

Imagine living into your 70s, 80s, and beyond as healthy as and with the vitality of people decades younger!

Today, there's a new, super-potent form of CoQ10 that acts as a powerful *vitality booster* and *improves your quality of life – making you feel younger and more exuberant.*

It's called ubiquinol, and it's an incredible EIGHT times more powerful than regular CoQ10.

Here's How It Works…

Traditionally, all CoQ10 supplements used the old-style ingredient *ubiquinone*. But once this gets into your system, your body has to convert it into another substance called *ubiquinol*.

Ubiquinol is the form of CoQ10 that works miracles. But there's a problem… Your body's ability to convert ubiquinone starts to decline after age 45. As a result, your body doesn't get the full effect. And in many cases – if you're 50 or older – traditional CoQ10 won't give you the chance to stay young into old age.

But Japanese researchers – led by my friend and colleague Dr. Mae – recently discovered a reliable way to skip the conversion process. So now, ubiquinol gets into your blood at super-high concentrations – with no effort on your body's part.

The idea has been around for some time. But until now, no one could figure out how to make it stable enough to take in this form.

Ubiquinol gives you eight times higher absorption and keeps your blood levels high over an extended period. High blood levels make all the difference. That's what you need to delay the effects of aging.

Have a look at the graph below. You can see the remarkable absorption power of ubiquinol and how it compares with the old form of CoQ10.

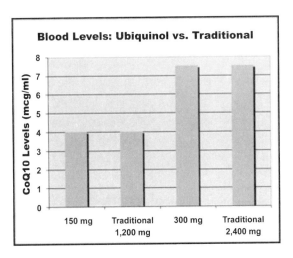

Blood Levels: Ubiquinol vs. Traditional

Just 150 mg of ubiquinol elevates blood levels to almost 4 mcg/ml. You would need 1,200 mg of the traditional form of CoQ10 to match that effect.

And when you double the dose of ubiquinol to 300 mg – you'd have to take a whopping 2,400 mg of the traditional CoQ10 to equal that power.

What may be even more critical is how long ubiquinol stays in your body compared to the old form. In one study using mice, ubiquinol was present in the blood at a 3.75-fold greater concentration after 8 hours. (A blood level of 4.5 mcg/ml after 8 hours of taking 100 mg.)

This high concentration staying in your system for 8 hours is one of the keys to its age-defying potential. The same amount of traditional CoQ10 dropped to a low level (just 1.2 mcg/ml) after 8 hours – too low to have a powerful anti-aging effect.

With ubiquinol you get all the benefits of regular CoQ10 – but on a much grander scale and much more effectively.

When my patients take ubiquinol, they become stronger, more energetic, and more productive.

And it's easy to understand why: For the first time in medical history, we have the ability to drive an unlimited amount of fresh energy to our cells — *every day*.

Supercharge Your Energy and Stamina

Thanks to a new study, we've confirmed that *ubiquinol improves your quality of life – making you feel younger and more exuberant.*

In the study, people taking ubiquinol showed a dramatic improvement in their "Vitality Score," and "Mental Health Score."

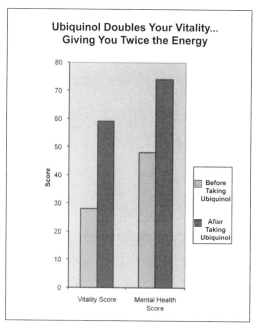

Here's what happened: Men and women living in a nursing home took ubiquinol for nine months. They were all between the ages of 69 and 87.

Before they started, they filled out a "SF-36 questionnaire." This is the best-known questionnaire for measuring your health status. It's been used in over 2,000 published research studies.

When these folks filled out the questionnaire a second time – after taking ubiquinol for nine months – the results were amazing: <u>vitality scores went up by over 100%</u>!

... Which translates into *stunning results that would NOT have been possible with the old form of CoQ10!*

When you take ubiquinol, you'll find CoQ10 in high concentrations in your heart, brain, and all your major organs. It's a powerful anti-oxidant that protects your organs and tissues from damage.

This means when you get enough of it, you can *re-energize your heart ... boost your cardiovascular health ... revitalize your brain ... and discover newfound energy and stamina.*

If you want to keep the power of youth into old age and feel like a teenager again, I recommend 50 mg of ubiquinol daily.

Better Than Coffee – Without the Crash

When I was hiking through the Amazon Rainforest last year, I had a firsthand experience with a remarkable healing herb.

Sacred to the nearby Guarani tribe, it was literally a gift from the gods. According to tribal folklore, the Indians of the Amazon River Basin have been using it to prevent fatigue and increase physical endurance since before recorded history.

I took it in the early morning before we hit the trail. After 18 hours of hiking through the jungles of Peru and covering 15 miles of rugged terrain, my mind was crystal clear and I didn't feel tired at all.

I realized that combining this ancient herb with cutting-edge brain nutrients would create a powerful new formula. Not only would it give you more energy without crashing, it would help your memory, too.

Kick Start Your Morning
Without Feeling Nervous or Jittery

The Amazon herb that kept me alert, yet relaxed, comes from a seed called *Paullinia cupana*. The active compound is *guaranine*, a member of the caffeine family. But unlike regular caffeine, it's full of healthy fatty acids.

The good fat gives guaranine a slow release. Its effect gradually increases over a period of hours. It doesn't pick you up and throw you down like quick-release caffeine. There's no crash with this stuff... and you don't get any of the nervous, jittery energy you do with caffeine.

The effect of the *Paullinia cupana* seed was amazing. It gave me the endurance to trek through the Amazon and left me with a wonderful feeling of clarity. But I was starting to see the bigger picture.

The Rainforest herb works its magic by releasing the neurotransmitter *acetylcholine* in your brain. Acetylcholine is the brain chemical that lets your nerve cells fire through the synapse or gap that exists between the trillions of neurons in your brain.

If you have lots of acetylcholine, your mind is sharp and your memory is clear. When you drink coffee in the morning, the release of acetylcholine gives you the buzz that gets you going.

When you combine choline and guaranine, you get a bigger release of acetylcholine – even more than when taking guaranine on its own. That's what gives you the feeling of energy and mental power. But instead of depleting your reserves and burning out, you build them up.

Sleep Better, Feel Better, and Even Think Better

Your brain has a huge appetite for choline. It's the primary building block for acetylcholine. You burn it up 24/7 as your brain uses it to maintain clear communication between trillions of neurons.

You need it for all the basics like thought, memory, and sleep. It even controls how you move. Your muscles receive commands from your brain via acetylcholine. That means your sense of balance and stability is controlled by this key transmitter.

Like many nutrients, your supply of choline drops as you get older. As this happens, you can expect some or all of these symptoms:

- Poor recall and memory loss

- Fatigue or lack of energy

- Brain fog and/or a sense of confusion

- Problems falling asleep, tossing and turning

- Unable to catch on, or learn new things

- Feeling distracted or irritable

- Walking with a wobbly or shaky gait, unable to stay balanced

When you blend choline and guaranine, it's like rocket fuel for your brain. Not only does it give you a better boost than your morning cup of coffee, it gives you the clarity of a mental giant.

You'll notice the lift right away ...

- If you do crosswords, you'll finish them in a fraction of the time. Things like organization, recall, and comprehension just fall into place.

- When you read something, you "get it." When someone is explaining something, you understand what they're getting at before they even get to the point. You move into a feeling of extreme alertness. You're aware of everything and it's all so clear.

- The processing speed of your brain gets a twin-turbo boost. It's like stepping up to one of those super-computers NASA uses for space flight.

To get the most powerful results, I recommend 500 mg of acetycholine (choline) and 250 mg of guaranine daily.

How to Turn on Your Anti-Aging Genes

You no longer have to sit around hoping or wishing you inherited "good genes." Today, you can play an active role in your own future by turning on the genes that promote longevity – and turning off the genes that tell your cells to die.

This isn't science fiction...

It's the cutting edge of what we call *nutritional engineering*. It gives you the power to decide which genes in your body get expressed or "turned on."

This is very exciting news... There's no need for excessive worry about your family history or whether good health "runs in your family." For the first time in medical history, *you decide* which genetic code gets played out.

When you visualize your future, what do you see? Are you playing tennis with your grandkids, or stuck in a nursing home watching TV?

The difference may be as easy as switching on the genes that keep you young and active.

Here's how it works and exactly how you can take advantage of this latest medical breakthrough.

Promotes Health in Every System in Your Body

New research uncovered a gene that increases lifespan dramatically. Every living thing on earth carries this gene – including you. And there's a nutrient that actually "turns it on."

It's called resveratrol.

Resveratrol is a powerful, "high-capacity" antioxidant that protects the cells in your body from early death and triggers the activation of your anti-aging genes.

Resveratrol switches on the genes your body naturally uses to extend life under conditions of stress (like starvation). They're called "sirtuins." They slow the death timer that's ticking in every cell in your body.

Sirtuins transmit signals to every cell in your body that cancel out the effects of aging. They bring the processes that lead to cell death to a crawl, buying your body more time to repair the DNA damage that brings life to an end.

For years we've been looking for a way to turn on these "longevity genes," and now we've found a way to do it.

In animal studies, resveratrol has been found to lower blood sugar and fight cancer, inflammation, and several cardiovascular ailments.

This gives your cells time to repair themselves – and live longer.

Resveratrol promotes health in virtually every system of the body, including the prostate, heart, and age-related brain conditions.

I've even uncovered a slew of studies *that haven't come out yet.* They add more proof to the long list of resveratrol's health benefits. Check these out:

- **Cancer.** Scientists discovered that it puts the brakes on cancer cells at every stage in their development. It stops the cells from dividing, growing, and spreading. Another found it works *with* UVB rays to kill off skin cancer.

- **Inflammation.** It protects the body from the effects of inflammation. Inflammation lies at the core of virtually every known age-related condition, from heart disease to arthritis.

- **High blood pressure.** Researchers in Japan discovered that it prevents the body from producing angiotensin, the hormone that causes your blood vessels to narrow.

You can benefit from the gene expression power of resveratrol right away. The problem is how to get enough of it.

I recommend adding foods rich in resveratrol to your diet. It's found in plums, grapes, blueberries, cranberries, and other plants. Wine and related beverages are a particularly good source of it.

Here's a list of high-content wines:

Beverage	Total Resveratrol (mg/L)	Total Resveratrol in a 5 oz glass (mg)
Muscadine wines	14.1–40.0	2.12–6.0
Red wines (global)	1.98–7.13	0.30–1.07
Red wines (Spanish)	1.92–12.59	0.29–1.89
Red grape juice (Spanish)	1.14–8.69	0.17–1.30
Rose wines (Spanish)	0.43–3.52	0.06–0.53
Pinot Noir	0.40–2.0	0.06–0.30
White wines (Spanish)	0.05–1.80	0.01–0.27

Foods, wines, and juices will help get resveratrol into your system. But as you can see from the chart above, you'd need to drink one to two *bottles* of wine *every day* to get even the minimum 10 mg per day I would recommend.

So resveratrol supplements are a better option. They're inexpensive and completely safe.

Here's the catch: not all resveratrol is the same. **You need the right kind to get the benefit**.

There are actually two different types – "cis" and "trans" resveratrol.

Every study I mentioned identified *trans-resveratrol* as the key health-promoting ingredient.

The problem is that the *trans* form is highly unstable. Research shows that it quickly turns into the *cis* kind when exposed to extended periods of heat or light during the manufacturing process.

That means it has to be kept in cold conditions and away from natural light. Otherwise that "trans" turns to "cis"… and you've wasted your money.

Pure, natural extracts that have been processed and stored in the right conditions are the best way to go. You can find them in health-food stores.

Proven to Reduce the Effects of 10 to 20 Years of Aging

In 1990, Dr. Daniel Rudman accomplished something that had never been done before.

He conducted a study that reversed human aging. Wrinkles disappeared. Gray hair regained color. Energy levels soared. And 70-year-olds had resurgence in sexual appetite.

He was investigating the effects of a pituitary protein called human growth hormone (HGH) on healthy adults. Twelve men, ages 61 to 81, volunteered for the trial. They received injections of human growth hormone for six months.

As we age, our skin grows thinner, we lose muscle and bone, and we gain fat. The men in the study developed bigger muscles, denser bones, and lost fat. On average, the participants experienced:

- 14.4% decrease in fat tissue mass
- 8.8% rise in lean body mass
- 7.1% increase in skin thickness
- 1.6% rise in bone density

When Rudman's study was published in the *New England Journal of Medicine*, he wrote:

"The effects of six months of human growth hormone on lean body mass and adipose-tissue mass were equivalent in magnitude to the changes incurred during 10 to 20 years of aging."

The Most Powerful Weapon in an
Anti-Aging Physician's Arsenal

Several other studies have now confirmed Dr. Rudman's findings. The benefits of HGH include:

- Increased energy

- Enhanced sexual performance

- Muscle gain

- Fat loss

- Stronger bones

- Diminished wrinkles

- Improved immune function

- Enhanced mood

- Decreased cholesterol

- Improved vision

While your body produces high amounts of HGH as a child, its production declines throughout your adult life. This decline causes and controls many of the changes of aging. When you reverse the decline of HGH, you reverse many of the consequences of aging.

HGH is FDA-approved for growth hormone-deficient adults, but conventional medicine has been on the fence when it comes to HGH. The concern is that we don't know its effect with long-term use. But the results of a recent 10-year study helped to prove its long-term effectiveness.

Researchers analyzed a group of men receiving HGH for 10 years. The men were compared to a group of men of the same age who did not receive HGH. The men receiving HGH had more lean muscle mass, less fat, more energy, and more stable emotional health than the men who did not receive HGH.

In other words, the benefits seen in the many short-term studies on HGH continued throughout the 10 years, without any negative side effects. The men taking HGH had appeared to turn back the clock, safely.

Boost Your HGH Levels Without Injections

You can restore HGH to youthful levels. I have researched the effectiveness of HGH through my Wellness Research Foundation and found that HGH can be elevated naturally:

- **Eat more protein:** When you eat high amounts of protein, your HGH levels rise. This is a mild elevation, but nonetheless, it's effective.

- **Perform strenuous exercises:** Strenuous exercise also increases levels of HGH in your body. I'm talking about gut-wrenching exercises here, like heavy squats and dead lifts. This is not a tip for the faint of heart.

If you want real HGH, it must be by injection, and a doctor must prescribe it. You must get your blood levels of HGH checked. If your doctor will authorize it, you can get a handy HGH cartridge for home use without needles. I've used it in patients from 35 to 95 years old at my Wellness Center in South Florida. I've seen some remarkable changes.

If you think you may be a candidate for HGH, talk to your doctor. Remember, it's only available by prescription, and to be used safely, you must have your blood levels checked. Also, make sure to deal only with a doctor who is familiar with HGH.

Overcome Tiredness by Countering Stress

While most hormones decline with age, cortisol – the stress hormone – increases with age.

Cortisol then plays havoc on your body by inhibiting maintenance and repair, which accelerates aging. It's like burning your candle at both ends.

DHEA, which stands for *dehydroepiandrosterone*, is the natural counter to stress.

DHEA is the precursor used by your body in producing sex hormones like testosterone, estrogen, and progesterone. It's produced in large quantities in youth, but its production dwindles with age.

You secrete DHEA when times are good – when you are well-fed, secure, and free of stressors. The more DHEA in your body, the less effect stress will have on you.

The problem is, your adrenal capacity to produce DHEA declines with age. Yet the modern environment stresses your body every day, and cortisol is overproduced and aging is accelerated.

People with DHEA deficiency have been documented to experience:

- Shortened lifespans
- Immune deficiencies
- Inflammatory diseases
- Cancer

- Heart disease

- Osteoporosis

- Depression

- Cognitive decline

- Aged appearance

A 1998 study published in the *Journal of the American Geriatric Society* studied DHEA's effects on aging. People between the ages of 60 and 80 were tested for DHEA levels. The participants also took cognitive and strength tests.

Researchers found that those with the highest levels of DHEA performed better on both the cognitive and physical assessments. Study authors admitted that those with higher levels of DHEA seemed younger.

Feel Like You Did Years – Even Decades – Ago

As I said before, DHEA levels decline as you age. The rate of decline is surprising. By the time you're 65 years old, you'll only have about 10% of the DHEA that you had when you were 20.

People with higher levels of DHEA experience:

- Less stress

- Enhanced energy

- A boost in immune system function

- Reduced body fat

- Increased libido

- Sharper memory

- Halt in wrinkles and signs of physical aging

You can raise your levels by: 1) Reducing your levels of cortisol; and 2) Supplementing with DHEA.

DHEA is becoming more popular as a supplement. I use DHEA at my Wellness Center regularly. DHEA therapy has successfully treated many of my patients who suffer from lack of energy, depression, and chronic fatigue syndrome.

It's important for you to get your DHEA levels checked. Your doctor can perform the simple test.

After your levels have been checked, you can determine optimal dosing. A common starting dose is 10 mg daily. DHEA is absorbed well and can be taken at any time, but best mimics the natural daily fluctuation when taken first thing in the morning.

PART 3
Build a Younger Body

Why Too Much Exercise Makes You Grow Old Faster

In addition to getting the right nutrients into your body, getting the right amount – *and the right kind* – of exercise is important to your overall health.

If you're doing a lot of long-endurance exercise – like long-distance running or jogging – I've got news for you...

These exercises won't reverse the signs of aging, and they won't build an ounce of muscle. Instead, this type of exercise causes wear and tear on your body. Your joints become sore, and your muscles become fatigued without getting an effective signal for growth.

Here's the good news: Research now shows that the right kind of exercise can turn back the hands of time. And the more vigorous the exercise is, the more effect it will have.

You see, like the telomerase activator and vitamins B12, and E, vigorous exercise makes your telomeres longer and stronger. And anything you can do to lengthen your telomeres serves to protect your DNA … and restore your vitality.

Recently a study of 2,401 twins found that physical activity was related to telomere length. Moderate levels of activity created much longer telomeres than either zero exercise or over-exercising.

In the study, the people got to choose the kind of exercise they liked to do. They did things like running, swimming, or tennis. Those who exercised moderately around 100 minutes a week had telomeres that looked 5 or 6 years younger. ***Those who exercised vigorously around 3 hours a week had telomeres that looked 9 years younger.***

The professor that led the study said, *"The act of exercising may actually protect the body against the aging process ... and people may actually look and feel younger."*

Of all the benefits of exercise, building and maintaining muscle mass is the most important ... and the most health-enhancing. This is particularly evident in elders – building muscle keeps you young.

Here are some strategies I've learned from sports training that have proven effective for building muscle in elders as well:

- Work the large muscle groups first (legs and back).

- Perform strength-training exercises only 3 times a week.

- Perform the exercises at high intensity for short duration.

- Progressively challenge yourself by increasing intensity and adding new routines to help stimulate muscle growth.

- Use slow and smooth movements to prevent injury.

On pages 39-41 I've included a table that identifies all of the areas you should address when exercising. But first, let me show you the best way to exercise for maximum weight loss, strength, fitness, and health.

Only 12 Minutes to Start Reversing the Effects of No Exercise or Over Exercising

PACE is my revolutionary fitness program that can burn inches off your waistline, enhance your stamina, and raise your energy levels in a matter of weeks. And it's the perfect type of program to get the vigorous exercise that helps keep your telomeres long.

PACE stands for *Progressively Accelerating Cardiopulmonary Exertion®*, and the concept is simple: short, progressively accelerated bursts of intense exercise followed by rest.

PACE makes it easy. In just a few minutes a day, you can lengthen your telomeres, build lean muscle, burn excess fat, and extend your life.

The types of exercises you choose are entirely up to you. If you have a gym membership, you might want to take advantage of their treadmills or stationary bicycles. If you exercise at home, you may opt for running, swimming, calisthenics … or even jumping rope. And if you're really out-of-shape, there's nothing wrong with starting out with a brisk walk.

Here's a sample 12-minute program chart:

Set 1		Set 2		Set 3	
Exertion	**Recovery**	**Exertion**	**Recovery**	**Exertion**	**Recovery**
1 min	1 min	1 min	1 min	1 min	1 min

Set 4		Set 5		Set 6	
Exertion	**Recovery**	**Exertion**	**Recovery**	**Exertion**	**Recovery**
1 min	1 min	1 min	1 min	1 min	1 min

I refer to each period of exertion followed by recovery as one set. Now, let's use this simple 12-minute program to get a better idea of how it works.

Look at the program chart above. Your first minute is going to be a period of exertion. For the first 60 seconds, you're going to exercise at a pace that you find challenging.

If you're new to exercise, or feel out-of-shape, take it easy for the first two weeks. The speed and intensity of your exertion should be fast enough for you to break into a sweat, but not so intense that you have trouble completing the 12-minute program.

After your first exertion period, begin your first recovery period. During your recovery period, slow down to an easy pace, as if you're walking.

You don't need to stop moving during your recovery. Simply slow down and go at a slow, easy speed. Focus on normalizing your breathing and tell your mind and body to relax. This gives your body a chance to rest and recover.

Now that you have a feel for it in your first set, simply repeat the process for your second set. Start your next exertion period and follow it with a recovery period. You'll soon get into the groove of exercising in short, vigorous bursts of activity followed by periods of recovery.

Try and do this 12-minute program at least 3 times during the first week. But each time you do it, slightly increase the intensity level.

With PACE, it won't take long to build up your stamina until you can really get involved in some of the more vigorous exercises that can really help lengthen your telomeres, like sprinting at full speed or adding weights to your routines.

To increase intensity and learn about some of the types of exercise that work best with PACE, see page 72.

---

10 Areas an Ideal Anti-Aging Exercise Program Should Address

As you get started in an exercise routine, there are certain areas that need to be addressed as you age. Here are some factors to consider when developing your anti-aging program.

1. **Metabolic Rate.** As you age, your metabolism slows down.

But just about any regular exercise – even walking 20 minutes a day – will raise your metabolism.

2. **Muscle Mass.** Choose exercises with weights that you can comfortably repeat 10 to 15 times. You only need to work each body part once a week to make a significant difference. For more serious training, your diet should include extra protein, and possibly supplements of creatine and glutamine.

3. **Bone Density.** Once you hit age 35, your bones slowly start to lose density. Weight-bearing exercise – such as stair stepping, backpacking, mountain hiking, weight training, or even tennis – help signal your body to retain bone mass.

4. **Fat Gain.** As your metabolism slows with age, you tend to gain more body fat. Ten to 20 minutes of cardiovascular exercise before and after breakfast will help burn this fat off efficiently. Exercising for longer periods will burn off muscle in addition to fat, and should be avoided.

5. **Flexibility.** Regular stretching exercises will help keep your body limber as you age. Beginner's level yoga or martial arts classes often teach excellent stretching exercises.

6. **Strength.** Training for strength is different than training for muscle mass. For strength, you exercise for shorter durations – 4 to 6 repetitions only.

7. **Growth Factor.** You can actually increase your body's production of growth factor by short, intense exercise followed by sound sleep.

8. **Lung Volume.** To increase your lung capacity, you must use

your lungs at their full capacity. That does not mean long, intense cardiovascular workouts, which unfortunately burn off needed muscle. Pushing a car for 10 feet, for example, is a much better workout for your lungs.

9. **Heart Fitness.** Ten to 20 minutes of strenuous cardiovascular exercise will build your cardiac reserve capacity. Stair stepping, bicycling, and swimming are much better than jogging. Start slow and build up.

10. **Coordination.** Leading a sedentary lifestyle allows your neuromuscular coordination to deteriorate. Exercises such as dance, sports, or martial arts counteract this tendency. But remember this principle: Don't play sports for exercise; exercise to play sports. Playing sports when you're out-of-shape can lead to injury.

When you exercise, remember to apply the concept behind PACE. Exercise in intense bursts for short durations, then recover. As you proceed, add extra intensity to challenge your muscles and your fitness level.

Show a More Luminous Face to the World

I've already mentioned that getting 10 to 15 minutes of sunshine a day is critical for good health. (Sunshine is an excellent source of vitamin D.)

But, it's a well-known fact that too much exposure can wreck your skin, by speeding up aging and even lead to more serious skin issues.

Plus, each day your skin is bombarded with free radicals, toxins, and pollutants that cause your skin to age. This results in lines, wrinkles, and sagging skin that can make you look older than your years. Over time, you may even notice brown spots and a leathery texture to your skin.

But there are ways to counter these effects.

One of the best ways is to nourish your skin with antioxidant-rich foods, lotions, and moisturizers. Antioxidants, used both internally and externally, will repair your skin – allowing it to renew and rejuvenate itself.

The Most Important Foods for Healthy Skin Are Ones Filled with Antioxidants Like Vitamins A, E, C, and CoQ10.

- **Vitamin A** is necessary for developing and maintaining skin cells. Without enough of it, skin gets dry and flaky, and may become prone to acne.

  Getting plenty of vitamin A orally, through supplementation or in your diet, can help keep your skin healthy and protect your skin cells from the effects of aging. I suggest taking 2,500 IU daily.

- **Vitamin E** is another great skin protector. You might be familiar with its ability to heal cuts and burns. But it also reduces signs of aging and protects your skin from the inside out. 400 IU of mixed tocopherols will add all the protection you need.

An Oil That's Great for Your Skin

Studies show that omega-3 fatty acids reduce signs of aging and protect your skin from UV radiation. They're also helpful for relieving symptoms of psoriasis and skin inflammation.

So add omega-3 rich foods like wild-caught salmon, tuna, herring, sardines, and mackerel for healthier and more vibrant skin, or take a fish oil supplement.

You can also get healthy omega-3s from walnuts, Brazil nuts, hazel nuts, and pecans.

The real show stoppers, though, are vitamin C and CoQ10.

- **Vitamin C** is crucial to the growth and repair of skin tissue and the formation of collagen. And now, the news has gotten even better.

  In a new study published in *Free Radical Biology & Medicine,* researchers revealed that vitamin C may, in fact, protect your DNA against damage caused by oxidation, which could lead to better skin regeneration.

  In the same study, they also discovered that vitamin C could also repair potentially dangerous skin lesions caused by mutagenic DNA.

  Clearly, vitamin C is one of the most important antioxidants you can add to your diet, and it's easy to do. Most citrus fruits are very high in vitamin C, and they make a tasty breakfast, snack, or dessert.

  So add some citrus to your day and start getting the benefits of protecting your skin's DNA and generating fresh, healthy, new skin cells. Or take in supplement form, up to 3,000 mg daily.

- **CoQ10** is just as important to your skin as vitamin C is. It's found in high concentrations throughout your body, supplying cellular energy and antioxidant power to all of your organs, including your skin. It counteracts free radical damage and prevents damage to collagen and elastin, which are necessary to keep your skin firm and young looking.

  If you're not getting enough CoQ10 in your food (and most people aren't), I suggest taking a supplement with at least 50 mg of the ubiquinol form of CoQ10.

Also, Look for Moisturizers, Lotions, and Skin-Care Products That Contain:

- **Vitamins E and C:** One of the first things to look for is skin-care products that contain vitamin E and vitamin C. As we've already seen, these vitamins are known for their antioxidant power. And both have been proven effective when it comes to the damaging effects of the sun (photo-aging). Vitamin C is especially beneficial when used on the skin.

  In a review of studies, researchers found that the evidence supporting vitamin C as a topical agent to fight photo-damage is conclusive.

  Results show better collagen production in treated skin, protection from both UV-A and UV-B damage, a reduction in the appearance of age spots, and a reduction in inflammation of the skin.

- **Green tea extracts** will also help to protect your skin from photo-damage and inflammation. Green tea contains a polyphenol called EGCG.

  In studies, people who applied green tea extract to their skin before going out in the sun experienced less oxidative stress in the skin. The green tea extract also reduced inflammation in the skin, which will help reduce wrinkles.

Choosing products with these ingredients will help keep your skin looking younger, smoother, and wrinkle-free. But there is another antioxidant that also plays a highly important role in the health of your skin.

For even more power, look for products that contain CoQ10, Teprenone, and Hyaluronic Acid. Here's why ...

Continued on page 46...

New Hope for Rosacea Sufferers

Tara Smith, ARNP, NP-C

One of my patients came to me quite frustrated. She was suffering from another rosacea outbreak.

"I've been told not to drink wine, not to eat chocolates, not to go outside," she said. "I'm missing out on all the fun, and I *still* end up a mess!"

I hear this from patients all the time. They feel like they can't do what they like. And they're tired of spending their hard-earned money on expensive ointments and prescription drug treatments.

They may reduce some of your rosacea *symptoms*. But they do nothing to cure the *condition*.

So, after you've spent all that money and avoided the things you enjoy, you're still gonna have the same problem. The redness, swelling, and acne flares right back up again.

But there is good news...

It turns out rosacea isn't just about the skin. Like most skin issues, the problem starts on the inside. Many times, it's the result of an imbalance of intestinal bacteria.

You see, researchers have discovered that many rosacea sufferers have an excess of harmful bacteria in their intestines. This creates a toxic environment. And it produces all sorts of inflammation, including rosacea.

It can also lead to digestive disorders, making it harder to digest your food. That may be why rosacea has such a long list of food triggers. Among the list are chocolate, vanilla, eggplant, spicy food, alcohol, and many more.

But your immunity is increased when you're able to balance the

Continued...

healthy flora in your intestines. And that, in turn, reduces inflammation and outbreaks of rosacea.

Here are some recommendations I make to my patients to help improve their digestive and intestinal health to prevent flare-ups:

1. Add a probiotic supplement to your diet. They're chock full of friendly flora that prevents the overgrowth of harmful bacteria in your digestive system and intestines.

2. Spirulina and other green foods promote healthy intestinal flora, too. Plus, they have chelation activity that binds to toxins in your body to help rid yourself of impurities. You can get spirulina in green drinks or capsules.

3. Many people who have rosacea and digestive disorders also have B-vitamin deficiencies. So start taking a regular course of B-complex vitamins. I suggest at least 50 mg of B-complex daily.

4. When you moisturize, consider a formula that contains rose hips. Rose hips are high in vitamin C that can strengthen your capillaries and help reduce some of the redness associated with rosacea. Plus, the omega fatty acids found in rose hips can help protect your skin cells from damage.

 *As a nurse practitioner,* **Tara Smith, ARNP, NP-C,** *has advanced training in diagnosing and treating illness. She earned her Master's degree from the University of Florida and became board certified as a family nurse practitioner in 2005. In December, 2008, Tara began working with Dr. Sears and has established a thriving practice.*

Try This for Lasting Beauty

Although I talked extensively about CoQ10 on page 18 and a little on page 43, here's more about what CoQ10 can do for your skin.

The outermost 10% of your skin (the epidermis) is filled with antioxidants that act as a barrier against the assault of free radicals and other environmental damage to your skin.

One of the most valuable antioxidants found in that barrier is CoQ10, also known as ubiquinol.

The level of CoQ10 in your skin is at its highest when you're in your mid to late 20s. After that, it declines steadily as you age.

Taking a CoQ10 or ubiquinol supplement helps keep your levels high. But you might be surprised to learn that topical application of CoQ10 can penetrate deep into the cell layers of your skin to help reduce the amount of oxidative damage to your skin.

In fact, the older you are, the more CoQ10 your skin will absorb. When researchers tested the effects of CoQ10 on two groups – ages 21-29 for one group, and 51-70 for the other – they discovered the middle-aged participants absorbed about twice as much CoQ10 as the younger ones.

Other research shows that when CoQ10 is applied topically, it protects the skin against photo-aging and oxidative damage to your skin's DNA. Plus, it also helps reduce enzymes that destroy connective tissue.

So when shopping for skin-care products, make sure to look for ones that contain CoQ10 – especially if you're beyond your 30s – to keep your skin looking young and glowing.

Reduce Your Skin's Age by 30%

Just recently, the groundbreaking research into telomere biology has advanced another step.

It's a breakthrough that can extend the youth span of your skin cells to reduce visible signs of aging. It has even been shown to reverse existing skin damage.

stance I'm talking about is called Teprenone, and it actively delays the shortening of your *skin's* telomeres and protects the DNA of your skin … so you can avoid the ravaging effects that come with age.

If you read the ads in women's magazines, you'd think the world is full of anti-aging serums that will make you look young, beautiful, and sexy. But none of the ingredients in those products can promote cellular rejuvenation the way Teprenone does.

The reason Teprenone is so effective is because it works on DNA – something other creams and moisturizers don't do.

In clinical studies, over a period of 30 days …

- 100% of the participants saw an improvement in sun spots and skin moisture.

- Redness and pore size were reduced in over 90% of participants.

- 75% of them noticed an improvement in fine lines, skin firmness, tone, and elasticity.

- It increased resistance to harmful UV rays by as much as 100%.

In fact, studies show that it can extend the lifespan of your skin cells by 30%.

By repairing your skin's DNA, you can plump up your skin and erase wrinkles, tighten up your sagging jaw line, make your crow's feet disappear, and reverse sun and aging spots.

It also protects your DNA in other ways. It prevents oxidative build-up in your skin cells and helps your skin produce natural proteins that protect against damage. And it protects antioxidant activity that keeps your skin healthy and glowing.

This is a real breakthrough in anti-aging and has the potential to change the face of skin-care forever.

The Ultimate Hydration to Quench Your Thirsty Skin

When you look at old pictures, you might find yourself surprised to see the beautiful complexion you had as a teenager. You probably still envision yourself the same ... clear, tight skin ... fleshy cheeks ... high forehead.

Part of the reason for that wonderful fullness in your skin was the presence of hyaluronic acid (HA).

You may have heard of HA before.

It's so effective at filling out your face that it's the key ingredient in dermal fillers like Juvederm, Restylane, and Radiesse. Dermatologists inject it into the skin to puff up your lips, neutralize your frown lines, and smooth out your skin.

That's because HA is the ultimate skin hydrator. It has the wonderful ability to attract water and plump up your skin. In fact, it can absorb 1,000 times its weight in water!

The problem is, as you age, the amount of HA available to maintain plump, healthy skin decreases. According to studies, this may be the reason our skin changes as we age.

Without enough moisture, your skin becomes loose, dry, and wrinkled ... adding years to your age. But when your skin has enough HA, all that water plumps up your skin.

It enhances both volume and elasticity to restore a youthful balance to your face, so you can start looking the way you did in some of those old pictures!

You can get HA injections to fill out your skin. If that's the route you choose to go, make sure to consult with a licensed professional who has experience with the products before making a commitment.

But before rushing to make an appointment, you should know that you can also get significant results using HA topically.

That's because your skin can absorb HA at a cellular level. Unlike some other moisturizers that simply sit on the top of your skin, HA sinks into the deeper levels of your skin tissue.

When you get enough of it, your skin will instantly become fuller, plumper, and more hydrated than it's been since childhood.

The fullness created by HA helps smooth away fine lines and wrinkles. And the added moisture softens, smoothes, and tones your skin for a more radiant and youthful look.

Stop Washing Your Face With Gasoline

If you look at the ingredients on just about every skin product on the market, from moisturizers to sunscreens to shampoos, you'll find health-threatening chemicals.

I'm not talking about chemicals that cause minor threats. These compounds pose real dangers to your health, including cancer. And, sadly they are FDA approved and labeled as healthy.

Check the labels on your shampoo, lotion, or sunscreen to see if they have any of the following: propylene glycol, parabens, PABA, PEG, or mineral oil. If they do, the product(s) may be doing your skin more harm than good.

Did you know, for instance, that mineral oil is a "by-product in the distillation of petroleum to produce gasoline"? And, that baby oil is just mineral oil with fragrance?

Johnson's Baby Shampoo "No More Tears" formula contains co-camidopropyl betaine, PEG-80 sorbitan laurate, sodium trideceth sulfate, PEG-150 distearate, polyquaternium-10, polyquaternium-10, tTetrasodikum EDTA, quaternium-15, and others. Does this sound like something you want to use on your baby?

Let's take a closer look at why you need to take some action to choose alternatives to what is being marketed to you.

The Skin Care Industry's Billion-Dollar Lie

Both my Wellness Center and my non-profit research foundation are headquartered in Florida, the sunshine state.

Plentiful sunlight is one of the main reasons people come here. Yet many of them – including a lot of my patients – avoid the sun like the plague. They live in constant fear of skin cancer. They hide out from the sun. And if they have to be in the sun, they think their only option is to cover themselves with chemical sunscreens.

This is somewhat understandable. The multi-billion-dollar skin care industry, with the help of the mainstream medical establishment and the media, has everyone convinced that the sun is Enemy Number One when it comes to skin health.

Here's what you won't hear: Sunlight is good for your skin and critical to your overall health and well-being. Get enough of it, and you'll actually reduce your risk for a wide range of cancers.

Continued on page 54...

Hair's Worst Nightmare

Anesta Dawkins

From Japan to Brazil, and all around the world… the latest craze is to have silky, straight hair.

TV commercials, billboards, and magazines are full of flashy advertising for revolutionary products that promise to "improve the quality of your hair inside out."

It all sounds wonderful, but at what expense? Has anyone ever stopped to figure out if it's really worth it? Plus, what's wrong with having curly hair anyway?

Well, let me tell you, you're taking a huge risk if you're using some of these treatments.

As a stylist and salon owner, I'm expected to keep up with the latest trends. I remember the first time I came into contact with one Brazilian treatment. I signed up for a special class to learn this new service, and it cost me a pretty penny. But on the first day, I had to run out of there. It smelled horrible! I find it funny now, but I'm so glad I was too sensitive to tolerate it.

Here's the scary part… I later found out that the smell was formaldehyde. Yeah, you heard me! The same stuff they use on dead people. Well, needless to say, there went that part of my income.

Okay, gals, let's keep it real. Formaldehyde is found in quite a few things like household products, cabinetry, etc. But to knowingly put that stuff on your scalp is totally absurd to me.

This keratin treatment from Brazil comes in the form of a liquid, so it's very difficult to keep it from touching your skin. After applying it to your hair, you then repeatedly pass a 450-degree iron through it to thoroughly seal the treatment. The fumes that are released during that process undoubtedly poison everything and everyone in the vicinity.

Continued...

And then you're told you can't wash your hair for several days. Can you imagine living with that obnoxious odor and spreading it around on your pillows, then onto your face?

Yuck!

After doing some research, I found out that you and your stylist should be forced to wear a gas mask and full-body protection... because what you're inhaling and absorbing through your skin can be fatal.

The EPA says formaldehyde is a carcinogen... which means it causes cancer. And according to independent experts on the Cosmetic Ingredient Review panel, cosmetic products should have no more than 2% formaldehyde in them to be considered "safe."

The problem is, a lot of these hair products contain 10 times that amount!

I also found out in my research that this original Brazilian keratin treatment is not even being distributed in Brazil. Hmmm...

Well I have curly hair, and I am most definitely interested in going straight sometimes. But after all I've been through trying to achieve that look, none of it sounds like a good idea to me.

My advice to you is to make sure you do your homework before making a decision.

1. Make sure your stylist is experienced in hair relaxing and chemical straightening techniques. If possible, get a recommendation from a trusted source.

2. Go in for a consultation prior to committing. Inquire about the brand they're using and if they test frequently for formaldehyde levels.

3. During your consultation, ask to see your stylist's qualifications. And don't hesitate to request information on how to contact other customers to find out about their results.

4. Make sure you completely understand the process and the steps you need to follow in caring for your treated hair.

Continued...

If you decide to go ahead and get it anyway, make sure you are well aware of the negative consequences that could result from the treatment. Not only the horrible smell and exposure to formaldehyde, but also what your hair may look like if things go wrong.

 *Anesta Dawkins is Owner and Founder of Salon Hottie in West Palm Beach, Florida. She's an accomplished hairstylist, platform artist, and instructor. With over 20 years' experience in the industry and a satisfied network of clients, Anesta is dedicated to keeping you current with the latest and most innovative products in the beauty industry.*

What sunscreens are very good at is blocking UVA rays. Yet even that presents a problem, because your skin needs exposure to UVA rays to make vitamin D.

That's a huge problem, because vitamin D is a vitally important nutrient that insures healthy function in just about every system in your body. Vitamin D's also the most potent cancer fighter in the world.

A report came out of a Nebraska university showing that vitamin D has the potential to lower the risk of all cancers in women over 50 by 77 percent. And in a study published in the journal *Anticancer Research* last October researchers found that sunlight – about 20 minutes a day for fair-skinned people, and two to four times that much for those with dark skin – can reduce the risk of death from 16 types of cancer, in both men and women.

Sunscreens rob you of all these health benefits. And that's just the tip of the iceberg. Here are a few more important functions sun lotions deny your body when they prevent sun from activating your skin's vitamin D factory:

Activated Vitamin D	The Problem	Vitamin D's Solution
Protects you from cardiovascular disease and arthritis	Your body is producing too much of a protein that causes tissue inflammation	Turns off the gene that makes it
Controls your blood sugar	Your pancreas needs to produce more insulin to control blood sugar	Turns on the gene to make more insulin
Regulates your blood pressure	Your kidney produces too much of a certain protein that raises your blood pressure	Turns off the gene that makes that protein
Helps prevent cloudy thinking and depression	Your brain is not making enough neurotransmitters	Increases production of the enzyme you need to make these neurotransmitters

Look for the Hidden Dangers in Skin Care Products

Not only do they block key skin-based activity that promotes health and well-being, but there are many common chemicals in most commercial skin care products that actually cause skin cancer and other serious health problems.

For example, many of them include a compound called PABA. This chemical increases photo-aging because it inhibits your skin's ability to repair cellular damage.

And get this: When studies were performed on PABA, it was determined that, in the dark, it's harmless. *But when you expose it to sunlight, it starts attacking your DNA!*

So while PABA may prevent you from getting a sunburn, it could contribute to sun-related cancers.

It also turns out that most sweet-smelling ointments, lotions, and shampoos are filled with something called parabens.

And parabens are **bad news**!

In females, they can lead to early puberty and menstrual problems. As women age, it gets more serious: infertility and breast cancer. In males, parabens can result in sterility, unmanly breasts, and excess estrogen.

You use these products on your body *every single day* of your life. And since your skin is the largest organ of your body, these nasty chemicals go straight into your bloodstream.

Once they get inside of you, they mimic estrogen, disrupt your endocrine system, and throw your hormones out of whack.

So I've been warning my patients about them. Especially since so many of them have come to me with hormonal issues.

Most of them are already aware that they need to stay away from hormone disruptors like plastics and pesticides. They also know to eat hormone-free chicken and eggs.

But nobody has ever told them that what they put **on** their bodies is contributing to the problem and increasing their risk of breast cancer.

The Top 10 Chemicals to Avoid Putting on Your Skin

Parabens show up on ingredient lists under any of the following names.

- Methylparaben
- Ethylparaben
- Propylparaben
- Isobutylparaben
- Butylparaben
- Benzylparaben

The list of harmful ingredients is long, and the names are hard to pronounce. But if you check the label, I'm sure you'll find several of them in your favorite brands. Here's a "top-ten" list of the most toxic types of substances in skin care products my Wellness Research team's identified – and the dangers they pose to your health:

Chemical Ingredient	Health Threat
PEG, polysorbates, laureth, ethoxylated alcohol	Potent carcinogens containing dioxane
Propylene glycol	Dermatitis, kidney and liver abnormalities, prevents skin growth, causes irritation
Sodium laurel, lauryl sulfate, or sodium laureth sulfate (sometimes labeled as "from coconut" or "coconut derived")	Combined with other chemicals, it becomes nitrosamine, a powerful cancer-causing agent; penetrates your skin's moisture barrier, allowing other dangerous chemicals in
Parabens	"Endocrine disruptors," these gender-bending chemicals mimic estrogen, upset your hormonal balance, and can cause various reproductive cancers in men and women
PABA (also known as octyl-dimethyl and padimate-O)	Attacks DNA and causes genetic mutation when exposed to sunlight
Toluene, also called benzoic, benzyl, or butylated hydroxtoluene	Anemia, low blood cell count, liver and kidney damage, birth defects
Phenol carbolic acid	Circulatory collapse, paralysis, convulsions, coma, death from respiratory failure

Chemical Ingredient	Health Threat
Acrylamide	Breast cancer
Octyl-methoxycinnamate (OMC)	Kills skin cells
Mineral oil, paraffin, petrolatum	Coats skin like plastic and clogs pores, trapping toxins in, slows skin cell growth, disrupts normal hormone function, suspected of causing cancer

Here's what you can do right away to stop poisoning your body with these estrogen mimickers:

1) Read the ingredients in your skin-care products just as carefully as you do your food labels. Avoid anything that has the word "paraben" at the end of it.

2) Look for products with natural preservatives. Some of the best are grapefruit seed extract, citrus seed, potassium sorbate, sorbic acid, phenoxyethanol, and vitamins A, C, and E.

3) Don't trust the "all-natural" label. Just because a product says it's natural, it doesn't mean there aren't parabens in it. So make sure you don't skip steps 1 and 2 above, even if a product is labeled all-natural or organic.

The Simplest Way to Give Your Skin a Radiant Glow

Your body needs sunlight like it needs nutrients. In fact, moderate sun exposure helps to increase antioxidants in your skin and does far more to prevent cancer than to cause it. Plus, it provides your body with a free, natural source of life-saving vitamin D.

But overexposure to the sun consumes and lowers the antioxidant levels in your skin.

I'm sure you've seen people with deep grooves in their face ... their skin looks like a dried-up piece of leather.

To avoid damaging your skin while outdoors, here are some helpful tips:

1) **A little sun goes a long way.** At the right time of day and year, it takes very little time in the sun to maximize the benefits to your health. At high noon on a summer's day, you can get a full daily dose of vitamin D in as little as 10 minutes, depending on your coloring.

2) **Obey the laws of good nutrition.** Watch your diet and eat whole foods. Get plenty of high-quality lean proteins from sources like grass-fed beef, wild Alaskan salmon, sardines, eggs, and chicken. Also eat plenty of fruits and vegetables. These foods not only protect your body against cancer, they also help repair any minor sun damage your skin may experience.

3) **Don't ever let your skin burn.** You should get sun gradually and consistently over a long period of time. If you're sensitive to the sun, you may start out by only exposing small parts of your body and building up to more exposure.

4) **Know your skin type.** If you have very fair skin and burn easily, you have a higher risk of skin cancer and photo-aging. Still, it's safe to be in the sun as long as you don't overdo it. If you have darker skin, you'll need to increase the duration of your exposure to get the full benefits of vitamin D production.

5) **Skip the chemical sunscreens.** Sunscreen prevents the formation of vitamin D. It also uses chemicals that may not be good for you.

The fact is, smart exposure to the sun can help keep your skin looking healthier and younger – and you'll also reap the many natural health benefits.

The Truth About What It Takes to Protect Your Skin From Sun Damage

People slather on sunscreen and head into intense sun for hours thinking they're safe from overexposure to the sun. But there's a problem with that line of thought.

What sunscreens are very good at is blocking UV-B rays, and your skin needs exposure to UV-B rays to make vitamin D.

Worse, most sunscreens don't block UV-A light. And it's overexposure to UV-A light that accelerates photo-aging of your skin.

When you spend a long time in the sun, unprotected from UV-A, this type of radiation can chemically transform and excite certain acids in your skin that then contribute to photo-aging, pigmentation changes, and wrinkles.

That's where **SOD (superoxide dismatuse)** can really help. SOD is the "master guardian" of your body's immune system and is your number one *primary* antioxidant. But you don't get it from the food

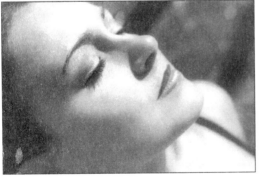

you eat … your body manufactures it.

You see, antioxidants come from two places – your body and your diet. The ones your body can make – like SOD – are the primary antioxidants and the most powerful.

Secondary antioxidants are the ones you get from your diet or supplements, like CoQ10 and vitamin E.

SOD doesn't just seek and destroy free radicals. That's what *secondary* antioxidants do. SOD actually raises the response of your entire immune system. This makes every cell in your body more resilient and better able to fight off attacks from the outside. No other antioxidant even comes close to this kind of power.

SOD zaps the destructive free radicals that form when sunlight hits your skin – and it powers up your immune system at the same time.

This means that when you power up with SOD, you can wipe out the damage of sun exposure and sunburn – and keep your skin looking great for years to come.

Take a look at what studies have revealed:

When dermatologists in France gave a new form of

Sun Protection in a Pill

When 150 people took the new form of SOD, Glisodin, for two months while keeping their sunbathing routines consistent, here's what happened …

They were split into three groups: 75 people who usually have significant flushing or reddening almost immediately during exposure; 60 who experience moderate sun reactions; and 15 patients who experience other reactions like irritated skin.

Results after four to eight weeks: 64 in the first group of sensitive sunbathers reported excellent tolerance to continued sun exposure.

In the second group, 44 had no experience of sunburn or negative reactions. And in group three, a full 100% of the people reported none of the symptoms they usually experienced with sunbathing. Overall, 82% of people judged their skin was well prepared for sun exposure.

This was an open study conducted in France on 150 patients by 40 dermatologists following a protocol compiled by Catherine Laverdet, MD, et al. Sponsored by ISOCELL Nutra, France. March 2005

Source: Matsumura, Y. *Toxicology and Applied Pharmacology 2004*

SOD to 50 volunteers for four weeks, the people taking the SOD capsule had a dramatic increase in the minimum amount of exposure necessary to produce sunburn.

Even fair-skinned people required EIGHT TIMES more UV exposure to produce sunburn than the control group. Since sunburn is the leading cause of brown spots and wrinkles, this is really big news!

Look for the new, advanced form of SOD called Glisodin to get these powerful effects. Where most SOD supplementation is destroyed in the stomach, Glisodin is wrapped in a protective coating to send it through your digestive track without being damaged.

PART 4
Live Younger Longer
Recreate the Body of Your Youth

Are Your Lungs Shrinking?

I bet your doctor never told you this… As you age, cells in your lungs start to die off faster than you replace them – causing your lungs to shrink.

That's bad news for your strength, stamina, and disease-fighting power. And here's the kicker: The smaller your lungs, the greater your chance of dying – of ALL causes!

But I have proof that it's completely preventable… even reversible. YOU can make shrinking lungs – and shortened "healthspans" – a thing of the past!

Powerful Research From Around the World Reveals the Deadly Threat of Lost Lungpower…

I began to see the connection between lungpower and strength back in the early seventies. Then, I discovered the pioneering work of Dr. Dean Ward, who uncovered clinical evidence connecting the loss of lungpower to aging. He even found that lung capacity is **the key** indicator of how long you'll live.

This should have shocked the medical establishment… But his observation fell on deaf ears. To this day, mainstream medicine continues to ignore the vital importance of lungpower.

Look at the graph on page 65… By the time you're 50, you've lost 40% of your breathing capacity! And that's downright dangerous…

Twenty years of clinical research all points to the same thing: Loss of lungpower spells bad news for your strength, your heart, your health, and your brain!

In 1988, the *European Society of Cardiology* reported that even a moderate decline of lung volume increases your risk of heart disease

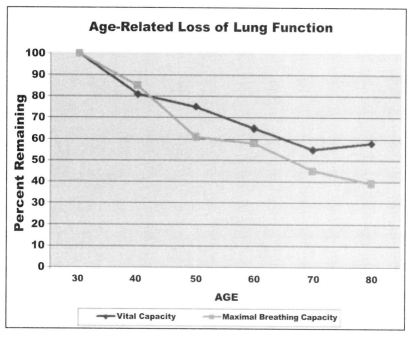

Adapted from "Biological Aging Measurement." Dr. Dean Ward. 1988

by 200 percent. This is true even for those who have no family history of heart disease.

In Denmark, the Copenhagen City Heart Study found that a loss of lung volume raises the risk of first-time stroke by over 30 percent and boosts the risk of fatal stroke by 200 percent.

When Your Lung Volume Drops, Your Body Can't Get Enough Oxygen!

A chronic lack of oxygen sets off a dangerous chain reaction: Your mind becomes foggy… your energy dries up…

Even the simple act of getting off the couch can leave you breathless… and your body becomes a helpless target for any number of deadly diseases.

Finally... **Aerobics Is Dead!**

The biggest mistake of the 1980s is finally over and done with... Jumping around for 45 minutes to an hour won't boost your lung capacity, it won't strengthen your heart – it won't even help you lose weight.

Even worse, aerobic training – the kind most doctors and even the federal government tout as the path to good health – can actually wreck your body. Do enough, and aerobics will make you sick, tired and old before your time.

Why? Because, it wipes out your heart's and lung's *reserve capacity*.

Your reserve capacity is what your heart and lungs use to deal with stress.

Injuries or physical trauma, a shocking emotional blow, a particularly intense session in the bedroom with your partner – these all demand reserve energy.

Reserve capacity means your heart has the ability to pump more blood faster in times of stress. Reserve capacity for your lungs allows them to deal with high exertion like lifting, carrying, running, or going up stairs.

Without reserve capacity, you're much more likely to drop dead from a heart attack or pneumonia when faced with stress. No "reserve capacity" in your checking or savings account means bankruptcy. No "reserve capacity" in your heart and lungs means a fatal heart attack or succumbing to what should have been nothing more than bronchitis or "walking" pneumonia.

But a different kind of exercise ***builds*** reserve capacity for your lungs, your heart and your blood vessels... and gives you many other health benefits as well.

Get Into the Best Shape of Your Life

Earlier we talked about my PACE program and how it can help you lengthen telomeres.

It can also increase your lung capacity, improve your cardiovascular health, and burn more calories … in just 12 minutes a day.

It can also give your heart the power of a 20-year-old. And with all that EXTRA strength and oxygen, you'll REAWAKEN the energy and vitality you had years ago – even if you're past retirement.

I've seen 2-pack-a-day smokers turn the tables on decades of lung damage… I've seen frail 85-year-olds regain their strength and vitality.

Plus, with PACE your troubles getting and *staying* in tip-top condition are over.

So you can say goodbye to:

- Hours of drudgery at the gym…

- Contradictions and confusion…

Is Your Heart Getting Weaker?

Every day the volume of blood your heart can pump gets smaller and smaller.

It starts in your 30s. And by the time you reach your 50s, you begin to feel it – especially when you exert yourself or encounter a stressful situation. Your heart begins thumping in your chest, your breath becomes ragged, and you have to take "breaks" constantly.

Worse, if your heart can't keep up … if it can't pump fast enough … you're much more likely to d*rop dead from a heart attack.*

And most doctors – even the AMA – are offering exercise advice that may be one of the **worst** *things you can do for your heart – weakening it instead of building strength.*

It doesn't have to be this way. You can give your heart the power of a 20-year-old. And with all that EXTRA strength and oxygen, you'll REAWAKEN the energy and vitality you had years ago – even if you're past retirement.

- Starting and stopping programs…
- Your most stubborn body fat…
- Frustrating roadblocks and plateaus…
- Needless pain and injuries…

And exercises that don't work…

In a matter of weeks, my PACE program will burn inches off your waistline, enhance your stamina, and raise your energy levels.

For years, people just like you have been discovering that, with PACE, they can take weight off and KEEP it off … in as little as 12 minutes a day!

What We Learned From Our Caveman Ancestors About Exercise

Admit it … exercising can be pure drudgery. You've probably pushed yourself hard at the gym, often times without seeing the results you wanted. When that happens, it's hard not to wonder if you're doing something wrong … or worse: feeling like you were wasting your valuable time.

PACE shatters all the misconceptions about health, aging, and fitness. In fact, PACE proves – beyond a shadow of doubt – that a strong, slim body and vibrant health does NOT have to be difficult, time-consuming or boring.

Just look at our caveman ancestors. They had incredible strength and survived under punishing and life-threatening conditions – but they didn't make themselves repeat the same movement 10,000 times – day after day!

So, what did cavemen know that mainstream medicine doesn't?

Variation.

Cavemen followed natural cycles of work and rest – or what I call periods of exertion and recovery. They didn't run for hours on end, starve themselves with ridiculous diets, or repeatedly lift boulders over their heads to build bigger muscles.

My patented PACE program taps into those same principles – with amazing results!

So, if you're seriously interested in losing weight, building muscle, and creating a strong and healthy body, here's my doctor-recommended solution for you: work out less and eat more.

I'm not kidding!

Your body simply wasn't designed for long, repetitive exercise. Instead, it was designed to handle short, intense periods of exertion, followed by rest.

That's the basis of my PACE program, and I'll bet you're wondering exactly how this works.

Let me clear up a few myths and misconceptions for you first. Then, I'll show you how you can incorporate PACE into your life for a slimmer, stronger, and healthier future.

Myth #1 –
Your Best Heart Workout Is Cardio Exercise

I can't tell you how many times my patients have come to me thinking that aerobics and long-duration "cardio" is the best and only way to improve their heart and lungs.

The truth is, cardio takes you away from your body's natural challenges. It's just not natural to repeat the same movement continuously without variation or rest.

Long-duration, medium-intensity workouts decrease your cardiac output and put more stress on your heart. Sadly enough, marathon runners have a 50% higher chance of having a heart attack.

It's time to face the facts: Cardio does not build heart health and does not correct what we are lacking.

Myth #2 –
Weight Training Builds Strong Muscle

Weight training is equally unnatural, ineffective, and misnamed.

Far from "training" anything, practicing these isolated tensing movements "untrains" your muscles. Instead of producing real strength that you can use in real situations, it produces bloated muscle fibers that become dysfunctional, injury prone and uncoupled from neuronal coordination.

Myth #3 –
Aerobics Builds Lung Capacity

Similarly, the concept of aerobics is a flawed and incomplete science that falls apart under analysis.

If you only exercise within your current aerobic limits, you do so without improving your *aerobic capacity*. In other words, you never push hard enough to stop to catch your breath!

This type of exercise trains your body for endurance and efficiency, which sounds great on the surface.

But this kind of "logic" causes "shrinkage": Smaller muscles, smaller heart, and smaller lungs. What's worse, it wipes out your heart's *reserve capacity*.

PACE Knocks Out Cardio in Clinical Showdown

Two of my most successful coaching students turned out to be a perfect illustration of how well PACE works – because they are identical twin sisters.

When they arrived for their initial assessment, both twins – age 18 – had almost identical body composition measurements. (Body composition measures the amount of body fat and lean body mass, or muscle.)

By the end of the 16-week study, the twin doing PACE was *sprinting* for 6 sets. Each set had a 50-yard interval followed by a rest period of 30 seconds. The twin doing traditional cardio was *jogging* 10 miles with no breaks.

The results? The PACE twin went from 24.5% body fat all the way down to 10% for a total fat loss of 18 pounds. What's more, she gained 9 pounds of pure muscle.

The cardio twin also started at 24.5% body fat but went down to only 19.5% body fat for a total fat loss of 8 pounds. And instead of gaining valuable muscle, the cardio twin actually *lost* muscle.

Overall, the PACE twin lost 125% more fat than the cardio twin, and gained 9 pounds of muscle, where the cardio twin *lost muscle*.

Of course, after this experiment the cardio twin got jealous of her sister's remarkable fat loss. So I put her onto the same program. Within weeks, she reversed her losses and soon slimmed down to match her sister's progress.

There's nothing unusual about this kind of achievement. I've reproduced it again and again. The twins did so well because I told them exactly what to do at each step in their program. All they had to do was follow along.

So, throw away your jogging shoes, cancel your aerobics class, and say goodbye to hours of never-ending workouts. Then round up all your "diet" books and toss them in the garbage...

You'll See and Feel Yourself
Getting Smaller, Tighter, and Stronger

Your first PACE workout will be a single period of exertion followed by recovery. You will start at a speed and level of intensity that feels comfortable to you. Then you will gradually increase your level of intensity until you are panting and breathing heavily. When you reach this level of exertion you will stop and recover.

This is the foundation of PACE. You start off easy, you gradually increase the intensity, you reach a level of maximum exertion, and you stop and rest.

To get started, you can walk, run, swim or choose an "instrument." An instrument is simply an exercise device like a rowing machine, an elliptical, a bicycle, etc.

If you are out of shape or not sure how you will react when you exert yourself then you might consider walking. It will be easier to control your speed and is a safe place to start.

As you progress you will have the freedom to improvise and make changes to your routine. There are many different ways to do PACE. You only need to use its principles. But your PACE will always follow this basic structure: You alternate between exertion and recovery, while making progressive changes.

Then, when you get the hang of it, you'll want to start "upping-the-ante."

During the 2nd week, you'll continue working at a level that's comfortable to you. But you'll also take the first step toward accelerating your exercise routine.

The level of intensity will depend on what equipment you're using. For example, if you're on a stationary bike, increase the level on the control panel so it becomes harder to pedal. If you're jumping rope or doing calisthenics, pick up your pace during each set.

To give you an idea of what the program is like, take a look at these exercises you can do right at home:

Jump rope. Your legs and your buttocks contain the largest muscles in the body. By strengthening them, you'll experience dramatic improvement in your overall functional strength.

Here's what a PACE jump rope exercise routine might look like:

	Set 1		Set 2		Set 3	
Warm-Up	Exertion	Recovery	Exertion	Recovery	Exertion	Recovery
1 min	45 sec	1 min	1 min	1 min	45 sec	1 min

Set 4		Set 5		Set 6	
Exertion	Recovery	Exertion	Recovery	Exertion	Recovery
30 sec	1 min	30 sec	1 min	20 sec	1 min

Squats also focus on your larger muscle groups. To do them, spread your feet until they're shoulder-width apart, push your hips back, bend at your knees, bring your arms forward, parallel to the floor, then squat as far as possible. Try to have your knees almost directly above your ankles, and don't allow for your knees to go over your toes. Return to standing position.

Try out this PACE workout, and you'll see results in no time at all:

Warm-Up	Set 1		Set 2	
	Exertion	Recovery	Exertion	Recovery
3 min (Stretching)	3 min	2 min	2 min	2 min

Set 3		Set 4		Set 5	
Exertion	Recovery	Exertion	Recovery	Exertion	Recovery
90 sec	2 min	1 min	2 min	30 sec	2 min

Each of these exercises takes only minutes a day, and will quickly and effectively melt off those extra pounds.

What Activity Tickles Your Fancy?

One of the greatest things about PACE is that it can be adapted to work with virtually any type of exercise available to you … from working on machinery like the treadmill, elliptical machine or stationary bike … to jumping rope in your own home.

Here are just a few that can get you started without a large cash outlay:

Calisthenics is a great approach to muscle conditioning, especially for those needing to recover from heart disease. By increasing the size of your muscles, you also improve stamina and stability.

Outdoor Sprints/Running is good for burning off calories while you preserve the reserve capacity in your heart. One of the greatest benefits is the ability to vary your routine and speed. Plus, when used properly with the PACE program, these sprints are great for developing lungpower and burning fat in the "afterburn" after your exercise.

Biking, like outdoor running, allows you to vary your routines. You can use flat, straight-aways to work with timed intervals, and increase your intensity by going faster. You can also change gears to make it harder or easier to pedal.

Jumping Rope is the best way to burn the most calories in the shortest amount of time. It's perfect for PACE and will push you to a higher fitness level, raising your metabolism and allowing your body to burn fat faster.

Some of my favorite workouts are done on **Stationary Bikes**. Whether you choose a standard bike or a recumbent bike, they're both great for working the larger muscle groups like the gluteus, quadriceps and the muscles of the lower back.

This kind of workout puts less pressure on your joints and improves your posture. Below is an example of a workout on a stationary bike for people who feel out of shape:

	Set 1		Set 2	
Warm up	**Exertion**	**Recovery**	**Exertion**	**Recovery**
2 MIN	2 min	2 min	2 min	2 min

Set 3		Set 4		Set 5	
Exertion	**Recovery**	**Exertion**	**Recovery**	**Exertion**	**Recovery**
90 sec	2 min	1 min	2 min	1 min	2 min

Your total workout time is under 10 minutes, with the whole workout taking only 20 minutes. Remember to slightly increase the intensity of each set as you progress through the routine. You can do this by ramping up the resistance on the bike you're using.

How to Teach Your Body That You Don't Need Fat!

Remember ... aerobics and other long-duration exercises like jogging and marathons create changes in your body that weaken your heart and lungs. They tell your body to make and store more fat.

This way, your body makes sure it has something to burn during your next aerobics class. And to cope with long-duration stresses, your body will actually *shrink* your heart and lungs.

PACE gives your body the right kind of challenge. And it only takes 12 minutes to get started! Not hours of grueling – not to mention boring – jogging and jumping around that most fitness "experts" tell you is the way to go.

By giving yourself the right challenge, with the right level of intensity, you get an adaptive response that tells your body that you don't need fat. And instead of shrinking your heart and lungs, your body will start to build vital reserve capacity – the kind that prevents heart attack and heart failure.

Fat Loss by the Numbers

Using my PACE program isn't the only thing you can do to build your dream body and get in the best shape of your life.

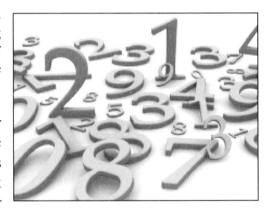

One of your best tools for fat loss is the Glycemic Index (GI). It measures how quickly foods break down into sugar in your bloodstream. High-glycemic foods turn into blood sugar very quickly. Starchy foods like potatoes are a good example.

This is important, because when deciding which foods to avoid, it's not always about sugar or sweetness. It's about "starchiness." In fact, potatoes have such a high GI rating they're almost the same as eating table sugar.

That's a problem, because foods with a high GI will spike your blood sugar. And when your blood sugar rises, it triggers a release of the hormone insulin.

What does this have to do with your weight?

Big spikes of insulin make you slow and tired, and tell your body to *make and store fat*.

There are other related problems, too. As a reaction to the rapid release of insulin, your blood sugar will often crash just as quickly as it spiked. This sudden drop in blood sugar will make you crave the same foods that spiked your sugar in the first place!

Some of the worst offenders are breakfast cereals, bagels, breads, white rice and potatoes. These aren't sweets … they're starches. If you take a look at the table beginning on page 84, you'll see they are all high on the Glycemic Index.

But there's one measure the GI can't give you, and it can make a big difference in your food choices …

A Powerful Duo for Helping You Make the Best Food Choices

I strongly believe in the GI and have been using it for years with amazing results. But, there's a missing piece to it… something that can take you a step further and give you faster, better results.

It's a tool most people haven't even heard about – the Glycemic Load (GL).

The Glycemic *Index* tells you *how fast* foods spike your blood sugar. But it won't tell you *how much* carbohydrate per serving you're getting. So it considers only the quality of the carbs, but not the quantity.

That's where the GL is a great help, because it brings serving size into play.

Why is this important? Some foods are high on the GI. Carrots, for example, rate a 92. But the amount of carbs in one carrot is very low. Carrots rate a 1 on the GL. So even though they are high on the Glycemic *Index*, when you take a typical serving size into consideration, their low Glycemic *Load* makes them a good choice.

Here's one that may surprise you. Corn rates a 55 on the GI. That's a little high, but would be fine in moderation. Until you look at corn's GL … a whopping 62. That means for every serving of corn you eat, you're getting a huge load of carbohydrate. That makes corn a very fattening food.

Together, the GI and the GL make a powerful duo for helping you make the best food choices possible to shed fat and keep it off.

Burn Fat Faster With This Simple Rule of Thumb

Different kinds of carbs have different effects on your body. But the fact of the matter remains … all digestible carbs are eventually converted to glucose in the bloodstream.

How rapidly that conversion takes place – and how long the resulting increase in blood sugar lasts – makes a huge difference to your health.

Here's something to keep in mind:

- The higher the Glycemic Index, the higher the spike in blood sugar the food will cause, creating an excessive insulin response.

- The lower the Glycemic Index, the slower carbs break down, releasing smaller, more manageable amounts of glucose into your bloodstream.

Natural simple sugars like those found in honey and fruit tend to be much easier on the body's glucose/insulin balance than complex starchy food. And foods like meat, fish, poultry, eggs and nuts continue to be some of the best foods you can eat. They are very low on the Glycemic Index.

Plain yogurt and most kinds of fruit are also excellent choices. The sweetness you taste from berries is a guilt-free pleasure because the total load of carbs will be low and they rank very low on the Glycemic Index.

Here's a general idea on how to interpret the Glycemic Index ... foods with a GI of 60 or above are high; those between 0 and 40 are low. Foods in the middle should be eaten in moderation.

The general rule of thumb I give my patients: Eat below 40.

A Simple Way to Hit Your Ideal Weight

Like the GI, high GL foods have a greater impact on blood sugar. A GL above 20 is high. Below 10 is low. Foods in the middle range are medium. Foods with a Glycemic Load under 10 are good choice - these foods should be your first choice for carbs.

Foods that fall between 10 and 20 on the Glycemic Load scale have a moderate effect on your blood sugar. Foods with a Glycemic Load above 20 will cause blood sugar and insulin spikes - eat these foods sparingly.

The Food Pyramid Is Making You Sick and Fat

The USDA food pyramid recommends that you eat grains, carbs, and starchy foods. But were we born to eat grains?

Farming and grain-based agriculture – the staple of our modern diet – were developed about 10,000 years ago. That's not a very long time from an evolutionary standpoint.

For millions of years before that, our hunter-gatherer ancestors lived on a diet of meat, wild vegetables, nuts, and berries. Their bodies evolved around a diet that gave them the strength, stamina and muscle growth for the hunt. And genetically speaking, your body is 99.998% identical. As you can see, not much has changed.

Our ancestors did something right. They followed a low-glycemic diet. Lean meats, nuts, berries… all low-glycemic. They developed this diet all on their own without books or charts. There was no science behind it. It was all they knew. And it kept them lean and healthy.

Rev Up Your Metabolism for a Hot, Sexy Body

Yarixa Ferrao

I've got a secret that can have your body working like a fat-burning furnace all day long. It's one of the easiest things in the world to do, and can help you achieve your dream body fast.

Eat small, protein-rich meals every 2½ to 3½ hours.

When you eat small, frequent meals, it allows your body to become a metabolic machine.

You see, when you don't feed your body often enough – or feed it the wrong kinds of foods – it starts thinking it's going to starve, so it goes into what I call "defense mode." And that's bad news. Because when this defense mechanism kicks in, your body begins storing FAT – the last thing you want it to do!

Now, I'm not telling you to fill up on pasta, french fries, and hot dogs every couple of hours. That's not the way to go.

Instead, to ramp up your fat-burning capacity, you need to eat foods that can be digested and absorbed properly. That includes lean proteins, vegetables, salads, and complex carbs – foods that are in a form closest to what nature intended.

The best thing about it: There is absolutely no sacrifice involved. You'll just get to eat a lot more of the foods you like.

Lean Protein: There's no need to stay away from protein. In fact, it's the one food that's really going to kick your metabolism into overdrive. When you get enough of it on a regular basis, your body has no reason to store fat. Try fish, poultry, lean steaks, eggs… and yes, you can eat the yolk, too.

Veggies and Salad: Eat as many vegetables as you like… the greener the better, but all colors are good.

Continued...

They may not have as much nutrition in them as they used to, they're still a good way to get the antioxidants and nutrients your body needs to feel satisfied and healthy.

Complex Carbs: Instead of getting your carbs from processed sugars and refined wheat products that pack on the weight, get as close to nature as you can. Stick with foods that are low on the glycemic index, like brown rice, sweet potatoes, millet quinoa, sprouted grains, and beans.

Here's an example of my daily eating plan...

Time	What I eat
7:00am	Water with lemon as soon as arising. Then 15 min. later, plain yogurt or kefir with berries.
10:00am	1-3 whole eggs with onions, red peppers, and spinach cooked with raw butter or ghee.
1:00pm	Salmon baked with coconut oil, on top of leafy green salad, olive oil and vinegar.
4:00pm	Whey protein shake.
7:00pm	Ahi seared tuna with squash and zucchini.
10:00pm	Kefir or yogurt, 1/2 cup.

Yarixa Ferrao, A.K.A, Coach Yari is a *Certified Personal Trainer (NASM) and an expert in functional training, fat loss, sports performance, and cellulite. Coach Yari is the founder of Get Fit in 6, a 6-week life transformation program for both men and women in Delray Beach, Florida. You can visit her at: www. getfitin6.com*

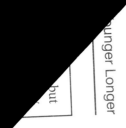

Glycemic Load will vary because they may use ~~zes~~. In the table beginning on page 84, I've in~~hat~~ reflects a realistic serving size - the serving ~~lso~~ included. You may notice when you look at ~~the table that meats~~ aren't included. Meat is carb-free so it doesn't affect blood sugar.

Ice Cream Anyone?

When making food choices, you need to consider both GI and GL because GI alone can sometimes be misleading. Remember … a food may have a high GI ranking because of the way its carbs convert to sugar, but the actual *amount* of carbs in the food may be so low that the overall effect isn't so bad.

Remember the carrot?

Here's another: Watermelon has a high GI rank of 72. Judging by GI alone, it would be a poor food choice. But its GL is very low, so while its carbs convert very quickly into sugar, there isn't much for your body to contend with. The overall effect on blood sugar is very moderate.

On the other hand, white rice seems okay when you just look at GI. Most brands of white rice have a GI of around 50. But they have a high GL, so even though the carbs in the rice may not convert as fast, there's a lot of carbs there for your body to deal with.

Pasta is another example. Spaghetti ranks a medium level GI, but its GL is very high, making it fattening if you eat it often.

Ice cream, which also has a fairly high GI of about 60, has a very low glycemic load – just a 6! That means the the amount of carbs you're getting from ice cream is small, despite the sugar. If you want to indulge, ice cream is a safe bet, but in moderation.

Here's another surprise... One ounce of a Dove dark chocolate bar has a low GI of 23 and a low GL of about 4. Who doesn't like chocolate? So enjoy this one too, in moderation of course.

There are many other foods that you may think of as sweet, and therefore "off-limits" – like fruit. Cantaloupe has a high GI of 65 so you might think it's off limits. But it has a low GL of 7.8. So, again, you are only getting a small amount of carb regardless of the sugar content. So try some sweet cantaloupe for a treat.

Simple sugars in moderation are fine - starches are a problem. You might think that piece of corn bread is harmless, but think again. It has a whopping 110 GI and almost a 31 GL. This one will spike your blood sugar through the roof. It's definitely one you want to avoid.

Tips for Fat-Busting Meals

To get the most out of your low-glycemic lifestyle, here are some tips to keep in mind when preparing your snacks and meals ...

- Avoid grains, including corn.

- Avoid potatoes and other white foods, like white rice, sugar and salt.

- Try making protein the focus of each meal. It kicks your metabolism into higher gear. All meats, fish and poultry are the real "guilt-free" foods. The protein will help you handle insulin better, build muscle and repair tissue—all essential for staying lean and preventing diabetes.

- Snack on nuts and seeds. They are a good source of protein and have omega-3s.

- Avoid processed foods, trans fats, caffeine, and high-fructose corn syrup. All increase insulin resistance.

- Choose vegetables that are low glycemic.

- Choose fruits such as berries and fruits you can eat with the skin on.

- Eat a high-protein breakfast every morning. It will stabilize your blood sugar and get you off to a good start.

Below is a chart I put together combining both Glycemic Index and Glycemic Load numbers for some of your favorite foods. I use it with my own patients.

As you review it, remember …

- The Glycemic Index (GI) measures how fast foods spike your blood sugar. High-glycemic foods turn into blood sugar very quickly. But the GI won't tell you how much carbohydrate per serving you're getting.

- The Glycemic Load (GL) measures the amount of carbohydrate in each servinge of food.

- A good rule of thumb is to stick to foods with a GI of 40 or below and a GL of 10 or below. Stick to those numbers and you will see results in no time.

Food	Glycemic Index	Serving Size	Glycemic Load
CANDY/SWEETS			
Honey	87	2 Tbsp	17.9
Jelly Beans	78	1 oz	22
Snickers Bar	68	60g (1/2 bar)	23
Table Sugar	68	2 Tsp	7
Strawberry Jam	51	2 Tbsp	10.1

Food	Glycemic Index	Serving Size	Glycemic Load
Peanut M&M's	33	30g (1 oz)	5.6
Dove Dark Chocolate Bar	23	37g (1 oz)	4.4
BAKED GOODS & CEREALS			
Corn Bread	110	60g (1 piece)	30.8
French Bread	95	64g (1 slice)	29.5
Corn Flakes	92	28g (1 cup)	21.1
Corn Chex	83	30g (1 cup)	20.8
Rice Krispies	82	33g (1.25 cup)	23
Corn Pops	80	31g (1 cup)	22.4
Donut (glazed)	76	75g (1 lrg)	24.3
Waffle (homemade)	76	75g (1 waffle)	18.7
Grape Nuts	75	58g (1/2 cup)	31.5
Bran Flakes	74	29g (3/4 cup)	13.3
Graham Cracker	74	14g (2 sqrs)	8.1
Cheerios	74	30g (1 cup)	13.3
Kaiser Roll	73	57g (1 roll)	21.2
Bagel	72	89g (1/4 in.)	33
Corn tortilla	70	24g (1 tortilla)	7.7
Melba Toast	70	12g (4 rounds)	5.6
Wheat Bread	70	28g (1 slice)	7.7

Food	Glycemic Index	Serving Size	Glycemic Load
White Bread	70	25g (1 slice)	8.4
Kellogg's Special K	69	31g (1 cup)	14.5
Taco Shell	68	13g (1 med)	4.8
Angel Food Cake	67	28g (1 slice)	10.7
Croissant, Butter	67	57g (1 med)	17.5
Muselix	66	55g (2/3 cup)	23.8
Oatmeal, Instant	65	234g (1 cup)	13.7
Rye Bread (100% whole)	65	32g (1 slice)	8.5
Rye Krisp Crackers	65	25 (1 wafer)	11.1
Raisin Bran	61	61g (1 cup)	24.4
Bran Muffin	60	113g (1 med)	30
Blueberry Muffin	59	113g (1 med)	30
Oatmeal	58	117g (1/2 cup)	6.4
Whole Wheat Pita	57	64g (1 pita)	17
Oatmeal Cookie	55	18g (1 large)	6
Popcorn	55	8g (1 cup)	2.8
Pound cake, Sara Lee	54	30g (1 piece)	8.1
Vanilla Cake and Vanilla Frosting	42	64g (1 slice)	16
Pumpernickel Bread	41	26g (1 slice)	4.5

Food	Glycemic Index	Serving Size	Glycemic Load
Chocolate Cake w/Chocolate Frosting	38	64g (1 slice)	12.5
BEVERAGES			
Gatorade Powder	78	16g (.75 scp)	11.7
Cranberry Juice Cocktail	68	253g (1 cup)	24.5
Cola, Carbonated	63	370g (12oz can)	25.2
Orange Juice	57	249g (1 cup)	14.25
Hot Chocolate Mix	51	28g (1 packet)	11.7
Grapefruit Juice, Sweetened	48	250g (1 cup)	13.4
Pineapple Juice	46	250g (1 cup)	14.7
Soy Milk	44	245g (1 cup)	4
Apple Juice	41	248g (1 cup)	11.9
Tomato Juice	38	243g (1 cup)	3.4
LEGUMES			
Baked Beans	48	253g (1 cup)	18.2
Pinto Beans	39	171g (1 cup)	11.7
Lima Beans	31	241g (1 cup)	7.4
Chickpeas, Boiled	31	240g (1 cup)	13.3
Lentils	29	198g (1 cup)	7
Kidney Beans	27	256g (1 cup)	7

Food	Glycemic Index	Serving Size	Glycemic Load
Soy Beans	20	172g (1 cup)	1.4
Peanuts	13	146g (1 cup)	1.6
VEGETABLES			
Potato	104	213g (1 med)	36.4
Parsnip	97	78g (1/2 cup)	11.6
Carrot, Raw	92	15g (1 large)	1
Beets, Canned	64	246g (1/2 cup)	9.6
Corn, Yellow	55	166g (1 cup)	61.5
Sweet Potato	54	133g (1 cup)	12.4
Yam	51	136g (1 cup)	16.8
Peas, Frozen	48	72g (1/2 cup)	3.4
Tomato	38	123g (1 med)	1.5
Broccoli, Cooked	0	78g (1/2 cup)	0
Cabbage, Cooked	0	75g (1/2 cup)	0
Celery, Raw	0	62g (1 stalk)	0
Cauliflower	0	100g (1 cup)	0
Green Beans	0	135g (1 cup)	0
Mushrooms	0	70g (1 cup)	0
Spinach	0	30g (1 cup)	0

Food	Glycemic Index	Serving Size	Glycemic Load
<u>FRUIT</u>			
Watermelon	72	152g (1 cup)	7.2
Pineapple, Raw	66	155g (1 cup)	11.9
Cantaloupe	65	177g (1 cup)	7.8
Apricot, Canned in Light Syrup	64	253g (1 cup)	24.3
Raisins	64	43g (small box)	20.5
Papaya	60	140g (1 cup)	6.6
Peaches, Canned, Heavy Syrup	58	262g (1 cup)	28.4
Kiwi, w/ Skin	58	76g (1 fruit)	5.2
Fruit Cocktail, Drained	55	214g (1 cup)	19.8
Peaches, Canned, Light Syrup	52	251g (1 cup)	17.7
Banana	51	118g (1 med)	12.2
Mango	51	165g (1 cup)	12.8
Orange	48	140g (1 fruit)	7.2
Pears, Canned in Pear Juice	44	248g (1 cup)	12.3
Grapes	43	92g (1 cup)	6.5
Strawberries	40	152g (1 cup)	3.6
Apples, w/ Skin	39	138g (1 med)	6.2

Food	Glycemic Index	Serving Size	Glycemic Load
Pears	33	166g (1 med)	6.9
Apricot, Dried	32	130g (1 cup)	23
Prunes	29	132g (1 cup)	34.2
Peach	28	98g (1 med)	2.2
Grapefruit	25	123g (1/2 fruit)	2.8
Plum	24	66g (1 fruit)	1.7
Sweet Cherries, Raw	22	117g (1 cup)	3.7
NUTS			
Cashews	22		
Almonds	0		
Hazelnuts	0		
Macademia	0		
Pecans	0		
Walnuts	0		
DAIRY			
Ice Cream (Lower Fat)	47	76g (1/2 cup)	9.4
Pudding	44	100g (1/2 cup)	8.4
Milk, Whole	40	244g (1 cup)	4.4
Ice Cream	38	72g (1/2 cup)	6
Yogurt, Plain	36	245g (1 cup)	6.1

Food	Glycemic Index	Serving Size	Glycemic Load
MEAT/PROTEIN			
Beef	0		
Chicken	0		
Eggs	0		
Fish	0		
Lamb	0		
Pork	0		
Veal	0		
Deer-Venison	0		
Elk	0		
Buffalo	0		
Rabbit	0		
Duck	0		
Ostrich	0		
Shellfish	0		
Lobster	0		
Turkey	0		
Ham	0		

Restore Your Youth and Vitality ... for Life!

Now that you're armed with the information in this book, you know there are safe, effective, and completely natural ways to protect and nourish your body and extend the length of your telomeres so you can stay young, radiant, and healthy ... no matter what your age.

- **Grow younger as you get older.** Get plenty of the right nutrients to maintain and lengthen your telomeres. Remember, telomeres are the key to anti-aging. Adding the powerful nutrients and antioxidants in this report will increase your chance of adding years to your life by extending the length of your telomeres.

- **Feel younger than you have in years.** Discover newfound energy and stamina by flooding your body with natural, life-giving foods and supplements that re-energize your body from the cellular level.

- **Rejuvenate your skin for lasting beauty.** The same nutrients that are good for your body can play an important role in the beauty of your skin. Not just by ingesting them, but also by using all-natural skin lotions and creams that are filled with skin-loving nutrition. And remember ... a little bit of sun each day helps increase your antioxidant levels while giving your body a radiant glow.

- **Rebuild the body of your youth and live a younger life** by getting plenty of exercise and following the glycemic index and glycemic load.

  And remember, you don't have to spend hours at the gym or run yourself ragged with cardio. Short, intense bursts of progressively intensive exercise will do more for your lungs, heart, weight and telomeres than long-duration exercise.

Don't wait. Use the information in this report to start your journey to a healthier, younger, and more beautiful you today!

References:

1. Reekie, Yvonna. "Telomeres Affected by Genetic and Nongenetic Factors." Research Brief. fr. *Focus Online: News from Harvard Medical, Dental, and Public Health Schools."* June 20, 2008.

2. Cawthon RM, Smith KR, O'Brien E, Sivatchenko A, Kerber RA, "Association between telomere length in blood and mortality in people aged 60 years or older," *Lancet* 2003, 361(9355):393-395.

3. Kaare Christensen, et al. "Perceived age as clinically useful biomarker of ageing: cohort study," *BMJ* 2009;339:b5262.

4. Kaare Christensen, et al. "Perceived age as clinically useful biomarker of ageing: cohort study," *BMJ* 2009;339:b5262.

5. Genetic Variation in Human Telomerase is Associated with Telomere Length in Ashkenazi Centenarians Proceedings of the National Academy of Sciences, November 9, 2009.

6. Xu et al. "Multivitamin use and telomere length in women," Am J Clin Nutr (March 11, 2009)

7. J.A. Vinson and P. Bose. "Comparative Bioavailability of Synthetic and Natural Vitamin C in Guinea Pigs." *Nutrition Reports International*, 27, no. 4, 1983.

8. Harper et al, "Resveratrol suppresses prostate cancer progression in transgenic mice." *Journal of Carcinogenesis.* 2007. 28(9):1946-1953.

9. Parker et al. "Resveratrol rescues mutant polyglutamine cytotoxicity in C. elegans and mammalian neurons." *Nature Genetics.* 2005. 4:349-50.

10. Philippe Marambaud. "Resveratrol promotes clearance of Alzheimer's disease amyloid-beta peptides." *Journal of Biological Chemistry.* 2005. 280(45):37377-82.

11. A Bishayee. "Cancer Prevention and Treatment with Resveratrol: From Rodent Studies to Clinical Trials." *Cancer Prevention Research (Philadelphia, Pa.).* 2009 Apr 28. [Epub ahead of print]

12. Roy et al. "Resveratrol Enhances Ultraviolet B-Induced Cell Death through Nuclear Factor-kappa B Pathway in Human Epidermoid Carcinoma A431 Cells." *Biochemical and Biophysical Research Communications.* 2009. [Epub ahead of print]

13. Gautam R, Jachak SM. "Recent developments in anti-inflammatory natural products." 2009. *Medicinal Research Reviews.* 2009 Apr 17. [E pub ahead of print]

14. Gautam R, Jachak SM. "Recent developments in anti-inflammatory natural products." 2009. *Medicinal Research Reviews.* 2009 Apr 17. [E pub ahead of print]

15. Brent C. Trela and Andrew L. Waterhouse. "Resveratrol: Isomeric Molar Absorptivities and Stability." *Journal of Agricultural and Food Chemistry.* 1996. 44(5):253–1257.

16. "Science of Resveratrol." fi. *Resveratrol for Life. The Definitive Guide to Resveratrol News, Advice, and Resources.* See http://www.seattle24×7.com/resveratrol/index.html

17. 14 Klatz, R. *Grow Young with HGH,* Harper Collins, NY: 1997.

18. Gibney J. et al., "The effects of 10 years of recombinant human growth hormone (GH) in adult GHdeficient patients," *J Clin Endocrinol Metab* 1999 Aug; 84(8): 2596-2602.

19. Klatz,R. Ibid p. 93.

20. Klatz R. Ibid. p. 93.

21. Adapted from Regelson W and Colman C, *The Super-Hormone Promise*, Pocket Books: New York 1996.

22. Cherkas L., Hunkin, J. et. al. "The Association Between Physical Activity in Leisure Time and Leukocyte Telomere Length" *Arch Intern Med*. 2008;168(2):154-158.

23. Stein, R. "Exercise Could Slow Aging" *Wash Post* 1/29/09.

24. Stein, R. "Exercise Could Slow Aging" *Wash Post* 1/29/09.

25. "Does the plasma level of vitamins A and E affect acne condition?" El-akawi, Z.; Abdel-Latif, N.; Abdul-Razzak, K. *Clinical & Experimental Dermatology*, Volume 31, Number 3, May 2006 , pp. 430-434(5).

26. "Gene expression profiling reveals new protective roles for vitamin C in human skin cells," *Free radical biology & medicine*: 2009, vol. 46, n1, pp. 78-87.

27. Eberlain-Konig B, Ring J. (2005) "Relevance of vitamin C and E in cutaneous photoprotection." *J Cosmet Dermatol*, 4(10): 4-9.

28. Farris PK (2005) "Topical Vitamin C: a useful agent for treating photoaging and other dermatological conditions." *Dermatol Surg*; 31(7pt2):814-17.

29. Katiyar SK, et al. (1999) "Polyphenolic antioxidant(-)- epigallocatechin-3-gallate from green tea reduces UVB-induced inflammatory responses and infiltration of leukocytes in human skin." *Photochem Photobiol*; 69(2):148-53.

30. "Comparative Topical Absorption and Antioxidant Effectiveness of Two Forms of Coenzyme Q10 after a Single Dose and after Long-Term Supplementation in the Skin of Young and Middle-Aged Subjects," *IFSCC Magazine* – vol. 8, no 4 / 2005.

31. "Coenzyme Q10, a cutaneous antioxidant and energizer," *Biofactors*; 2008 vol. 9(2-4): 371-378.

32. Topical Use of Teprenone. Study for patent WO 2006/120646, Sederma, Inc. 2009

33. Topical Use of Teprenone. Study for patent WO 2006/120646, Sederma, Inc. 2009

34. Topical Use of Teprenone. Study for patent WO 2006/120646, Sederma, Inc. 2009

35. "Age-dependent changes of hyaluronan in human skin," *J Invest Dermatol*; 1994 Mar; 102(3):385-9.

36. "Absorption of hyaluronan applied to the surface of intact skin," *Journal of Investigative Dermatology*, 1999, vol. 113; 740-746.

37. Lappe et al, "Vitamin D Status in a Rural Postmenopausal Female Population," *Journal of the American College of Nutrition*, 2006; 25(5):395-402.

38. Grant WB et al, "The association of solar ultraviolet B (UVB) with reducing risk of cancer: multifactorial ecologic analysis of geographic variation in age-adjusted cancer mortality rates," *Anticancer Research*, 2006; 26:2687-2700.

39. "Sunlight-induced mutagenicity of a common sunscreen ingredient," Department of Biochemistry, South Parks Road, Oxford, OX1 3QU, UK; John Knowland, Edward A McKenzie, Peter J McHugh and Nigel A Cridland.

40. "Epidermal trans-urocanic acid and the UV-A induced photoaging of the skin," *Proc Natl Acad Sci USA*, 1998; 95(18) 10576-78.

41. Mac-Mary, M. Sainthillier, J. et al. "Evaluation of the Effect of GliSODin on the Intensity of Actinic Erythema," presented at the CARD (Annual Congress of Dermatological Research) meeting in Brest, France, May 28th 2005.

Additional Health Resources

▶ **Power for Healthy Living**

www.alsearsmd.com

No one cares about your health and the health of your loved ones more than you do. We believe that the best way to ensure quality in healthcare is to allow you to be in control. We believe you have an inherent right to decide on the quality, expertise, respect and alternative treatments you receive for your own health. Live a healthier life with natural remedies and natural cures to help you prevent disease. Take control of your health and wellness now!

▶ **P.A.C.E – The 12-Minute Fitness Revolution**

www.pacerevolution.com

Dr. Sears' P.A.C.E. programe overturns accepted dogma and reveals a more effective, more exhilarating path to a strong heart, robust lungs and a naturally lean and effortlessly energetic body.

You don't need gyms, expensive equipment or high-priced trainers. P.A.C.E. is accessible to anyone regardless of age or current level of fitness. And it only takes 12 minutes a day.

Join the P.A.C.E. Revolution. Thousands already have.

▶ **Become a Patient**

Dr. Sears' Center for Health & Wellness offers the latest cutting-edge breakthroughs to keep you feeling energetic, capable and vital for as long as possible. He has personalized programs for men *and* women designed to improve your health. To make an appointment to become one of Dr. Sear's patients in Royal Palm Beach, Florida, you can call 561-784-7852.

▶ Dr. Sears' Primal Force Supplements

www.primalforce.net

Rediscover your primal energy and native strength with Dr. Sears' supplement line. Primal Force is the ONLY force that rebuilds you the way nature intended ... strong, powerful, healthy and energetic.

▶ Pure Radiance – Nutrition for Ageless Beauty

www.mypureradiance.com

You shouldn't have to sacrifice your health or risk disease for the sake of looking and feeling good. But your choices for clean, effective skin care are remarkably slim. Dr. Sears founded Pure Radiance to change that. Now you have real options.

Pure Radiance products are a completely natural blend of today's most powerful nutrients for healthy, glowing skin. Developed as the "New Technology for Younger Skin," this skin care line breaks away from the tradition of using parabens, carcinogens, pollutants and gasoline distillates that are commonly found in most of today's cosmetics and skin care solutions.

As an anti-aging physician, nutritionist and researcher, Dr. Sears believes total wellness and integrative health are found on the inside *and* out. According to Dr. Sears, "Your skin is one of the largest organs of your body, and if maintained properly with effective skincare, it can lead to an overall healthier and younger lifestyle."

▶ **Telomerase Activation**

www.telomeraseactivation.org

Finally, the first step toward agelessness has come! Imagine living to be over 100 years old, while maintaining all the strength and vitality you had when you were in your 30s. Leading a rich, active life, enjoying new hobbies and pursuits, playing outdoors with your great-grandchildren ... all without having to worry about age-related conditions like heart disease, chronic illness, fading mental powers, impotence, eyesight and hearing loss, low energy, and weak, inflexible muscles and joint pain. Learn more!

▶ **American Academy of Anti-Aging Medicine**

www.worldhealth.net/

This is the leading anti-aging portal for advanced medicine and preventative healthcare. Call **1-888-997-0112** or visit the website for the directory to search for anti-aging physicians, clinics, spas and products.

▶ **Get Fit in 6 with Coach Yari**

www.getfitin6.com

Fitness, nutrition and health expert Coach Yari gives you the truth about how to get into the best shape of your life. In six weeks you can look better, feel better, shed those unwanted pounds and get the body of your dreams!